The Words and Music of Taylor Swift

THE PRAEGER SINGER-SONGWRITER COLLECTION

The Words and Music of Taylor Swift

James E. Perone

James E. Perone, Series Editor

 PRAEGER™

An Imprint of ABC-CLIO, LLC

Santa Barbara, California • Denver, Colorado

Library of Congress Cataloging-in-Publication Data

Names: Perone, James E. author.
Title: The words and music of Taylor Swift / James E. Perone.
Description: Santa Barbara, California : Praeger, 2017. | Series: Praeger
    singer-songwriter collection | Includes bibliographical references and index.
Identifiers: LCCN 2017010646 (print) | LCCN 2017010760 (ebook) | ISBN
    9781440852947 (hardcopy : alk. paper) | ISBN 9781440852954 (ebook)
Subjects: LCSH: Swift, Taylor, 1989—Criticism and interpretation. | Country
    music—2001-2010—History and criticism. | Popular music—United States—
    2011-2020—History and criticism.
Classification: LCC ML420.S968 P47 2017 (print) | LCC ML420.S968 (ebook) |
    DDC 782.421642092—dc23
LC record available at https://lccn.loc.gov/2017010646

ISBN: 978-1-4408-5294-7
EISBN: 978-1-4408-5295-4

21 20 19 18 17   1 2 3 4 5

This book is also available as an eBook.

Praeger
An Imprint of ABC-CLIO, LLC

ABC-CLIO, LLC
130 Cremona Drive, P.O. Box 1911
Santa Barbara, California 93116-1911
www.abc-clio.com

This book is printed on acid-free paper ∞

Manufactured in the United States of America

Contents

Series Foreword

Although the term "singer-songwriter" might most frequently be associated with a cadre of musicians of the early 1970s such as Paul Simon, James Taylor, Carly Simon, Joni Mitchell, Cat Stevens, and Carole King, the Praeger Singer-Songwriter Collection defines singer-songwriters more broadly, both in terms of style and time period. The series includes volumes on musicians who have been active from approximately the early 1960s through the present. Musicians who write and record in folk, rock, soul, hip-hop, country, and various hybrids of these styles are represented.

What do the individuals included in this series have in common? Some have never collaborated as writers, whereas others have, but all have written and recorded commercially successful and/or historically important words and lyrics at some point in their careers.

The authors who contribute to the series also exhibit diversity. Some are scholars who are trained primarily as musicians, whereas others have such areas of specializations as American studies, history, sociology, popular culture studies, literature, and rhetoric. The authors share a high level of scholarship, accessibility in their writing, and a true insight into the work of the artists they study. The authors are also focused on the output of their subjects and how it relates to their subjects' biographies and the society around them; however, biography in and of itself is not a major focus of the books in this series.

Given the diversity of the musicians who are the subject of the books in this series, and given the diversity of viewpoint of the authors, volumes in the series differ from book to book. All, however, are organized chronologically around the compositions and recordings of their subjects. All of the books in the series also serve as listeners' guides to the music of their subjects, making them companions to the artists' recorded output.

James E. Perone
Series Editor

Acknowledgments

As has been the case for all of the writing that I have done for Praeger Publishers, I am indebted to the Praeger acquisitions and editorial staff as well as to the copyeditors with whom they contract. I am grateful that this well-oiled machine raises questions that I had not considered, provides such a keen eye to help find every uncrossed *t* and undotted *i*, and manages to make the entire process as smooth as possible.

I would also like to acknowledge the help of my colleagues Dr. Malynnda Johnson and Dr. Len Cooper of the Department of Communication at the University of Mount Union. Drs. Johnson and Cooper pointed me in the direction of some pertinent research related to celebrities' use of social media, something that has been at the heart of Taylor Swift's promotion and her relationship with her fans over the course of her entire career.

Finally, I thank my wife, Karen, for all of her support throughout this and all of my past writing projects.

Introduction

OVERVIEW OF TAYLOR SWIFT'S LIFE, CAREER, AND IMPACT

Easily the most commercially successful artist of her generation, Taylor Swift was born in Reading, Pennsylvania, in 1989, a fact that later inspired her album *1989*. Swift's family moved to Wyomissing, Pennsylvania, where they owned a Christmas tree farm. Swift demonstrated musical talent at a young age, so much so that by the age of 11 she had performed "The Star-Spangled Banner" at an NBA professional basketball game. Soon thereafter, Swift learned to play the guitar and began writing songs.

Early in her teen years, Swift visited Nashville to try to secure a contract as a singer-songwriter. Swift's family eventually moved to Henderson, Tennessee, so that Swift could pursue a musical career in earnest. Swift soon secured a contract with Big Machine Records and in 2006 released her first single, "Tim McGraw." Swift helped with the promotion of the song, including through her use of MySpace. This started an association with social media that continues through the present. Swift has used Twitter, MySpace, Facebook, and other social media outlets to connect with fans, to promote and release new songs, to comment on the work of other artists, and so on, as will be detailed later in this book.

Swift's late 2006 debut album, *Taylor Swift*, the singles it spawned, and her sophomore album, *Fearless*, and its singles all entered the upper reaches of the U.S. country and pop charts and established Swift—still a teenager—as a star. Swift's works from the late 2000s to the present have also generated positive critical reviews and a still-increasing number of Grammy Award nominations and wins. She is, for example, at the time of this writing, the only female artist ever to record multiple Album of the Year wins.

Swift's work may have started out in the country genre—certainly Dobros and banjos were a regular part of the instrumental texture—but the early references to alternative rock, hip-hop, and other genres suggested that Swift might be a singer-songwriter who potentially could go out of her way to defy genres. Swift's 2012 album *Red* was marketed as a country collection and received a Grammy nomination for Best Country Album, but some of her collaborative work on *Red* even more clearly suggested the influence of pop, alternative rock, and other hybrid styles. The 2014 album *1989*, which Swift named for the year of her birth, found synthesizers and dance rhythm tracks replacing the Dobros, banjos, and acoustic guitars of Swift's earlier work.

Interestingly, Swift had established a pattern of releasing new albums every two years, early in her career. These album releases also seemed to be tied to various relationships that had ended and that provided Swift with fresh inspiration to write new songs. Given what the media had reported about the ups and downs of Swift's personal life after the release of *1989* in the year 2014, it seems natural that fans would anticipate a new album in 2016. There was no new 2016 album for Swift, and at the time of this writing in early 2017, *1989* has not been followed up. Instead, Swift gave a number of high-profile live and televised performances in 2015 and 2016 and returned to her roots as a songwriter—her family had after all initially moved to Nashville when Swift was a teenager so that she could pursue a career as a professional songwriter. Swift wrote the song "This Is What You Came For" for her ex-boyfriend Calvin Harris, who recorded it in collaboration with the singer Rihanna. The Harris recording gave Swift an assumed name. Swift also wrote "Better Man" for the group Little Big Town. In the case of "Better Man," her identity as the song's composer was not revealed until "nearly two weeks after its release," according to Elias Leight of *Billboard* magazine.[1] There seems to be an element of the stealthy work of the singer-songwriter-guitarist Prince in Taylor Swift's 2016 compositional work, but perhaps she is testing the waters for returning back to her songwriting roots; only time will tell.

Taylor Swift's work has not just sold in droves and rekindled interest in the album as a unified whole during the track-oriented, playlist age, the packaging of the CD releases of her albums has rekindled interest in purchasing music in a physical medium during a time period in which conventional wisdom would suggest that downloading music was the new norm and that the CD was a relic of the end of the 20th century.

Although proclamations from pop music critics can sometimes rightfully be subjected to charges of hyperbole, it should be noted that Taylor Swift has been described as the "voice of her generation" by both fans and Yahoo Music writer Chris Willman.[2] In particular, because Swift's canon includes a fair number of songs in which she portrays social outsiders—particularly in her high-school related songs—or those who have been the victims of meanness, some of Swift's songs have resonated with victims of bullying. Her song "Mean," in particular, has been held up by advocates for victims of bullying as an example of a song of empowerment. Despite the fact that some feminists question the feminism of Swift's output, some of her songs are seen by other fans and other commentators as strong, effective examples of female empowerment.[3] Interestingly, the reactions of some feminists to celebrities such as Taylor Swift and Gwyneth Paltrow parallel the battles that surrounded the 2015–2016 campaigns of Bernie Sanders and Hillary Clinton, with younger women who considered themselves to be feminists supporting Sanders in large numbers and old-school feminist figures such as Gloria Steinem and Madeleine Albright supporting Clinton.

At the core of Taylor Swift's work as a singer-songwriter, however, is a keen awareness of and talent for creating memorable and commercially appealing melodic and lyrical hooks. The tunes in the choruses of Swift's compositions tend to be instantly recognizable and possess an intangible appeal that—as demonstrated by Swift's audience demographics—defies genre and audience boundaries. At their best, Swift's lyrics focus on familiar themes of love, loss in love (she has written quite a few of these), and alienation, but with these time-tested themes expressed in poetry that includes unusual—and highly memorable—turns of phrase.

Throughout her career, Taylor Swift has made no secret of the fact that many of her songs about relationships-gone-bad are autobiographical. Swift's CD booklets are noted for the fact that they contain thinly "coded" messages that reveal details about the relationships and even the names of some of the boys and men who jilted her. Swift's continuing string of failed relationships may have provided fodder for much of her best-selling and best-known songs, but it has also become something of the butt of jokes and even the object of money-making schemes. Richard Washington's June 27, 2016, article at CNBC.com, " 'Swifties' Take a Gamble on Taylor's Love in Chinese Online Marketplace," for example, concerns a Chinese gambling operation that allows Taylor Swift fans to place bets on how long Swift's relationship with Tom Hiddleston will last.[4] As a sidebar, apparently it did not. The deeply personal nature of so many of Taylor Swift's songs is not only fodder for comedians or oddsmakers, but it also ties her work to the early 1970s singer-songwriter movement. Interestingly, many fans of pop music consider James Taylor's 1970 breakthrough album *Sweet Baby James* as, in the words of the editors of *Rolling Stone* magazine, "the album that started everything" in terms of the confessional singer-songwriter movement.[5] Ironically, Taylor Swift is named after James Taylor. It should also be remembered that, like the jokes that Swift's relationship with Tom Hiddleston generated because of the confessional nature of Swift's lyrics, the earliest well-known songs of James Taylor generated ridicule in some pop music critics, notably the well-known Lester Bangs, who basically claimed that the early 1970s confessional singer-songwriter movement, perhaps best personified by James Taylor, led to the death of rock and roll.[6]

Still, despite some people's misgivings about the deeply personal nature of Swift's work, Taylor Swift remains one of the most successful singer-songwriters of the 21st century, an artist who is appreciated by those who are not necessarily hard-core fans, as someone who actually writes virtually all of her own material, an artist who stands up for the intellectual property rights of other artists, and as a woman who increasingly stands up through songs and in public forums as a champion of the underdog, the bullied, and the oppressed.

In considering Swift, her life and her work, it should also be noted that Taylor Swift is a pop culture icon who has (to use an old saw) put her money (and her time) where her mouth is. Swift has visited sick fans in their hospital rooms and has connected with individual fans with serious ailments through social media. She has demonstrated a commitment to her fellow artists not only by taking on Apple Computer's streaming music service, Spotify, and other corporations but also by donating $250,000 to the singer Kesha to aid her in her fight against her former manager and record company. Most recently, Swift's philanthropy includes making a donation of $1 million to aid in relief and recovery efforts in Louisiana after the devastating floods of August 2016.

ORGANIZATION OF THIS BOOK

As suggested by its title, the focus of *The Words and Music of Taylor Swift* is on the music, lyrics, and recordings of Taylor Swift, and not on her biography. That being said, throughout her career Swift has made both oblique and clear autobiographical references in her songs. In fact, she has widely described her early work as musical diary entries, implying an intimate tie between her musical output and her personal life. Because Swift readily admits the autobiographical influences that continue to be found in her work, I will explore possible autobiographical references in Swift's songs; however, my focus will be more global and more universal: What do Taylor Swift's words and music tell us about the characters that populate her songs, what they represent in the larger world, and how and in what ways they resonate with music fans and the general public? Discussion and analysis of Swift's music are arranged chronologically and are organized around Swift's albums. I have also included a chapter on Swift's compositions for other performers and other performers' covers of Swift's work, a chapter that focuses on Swift's career in the context of 21st-century technology—particularly her association with and use of social media, a chapter on Swift's work outside of music, and an annotated discography and annotated bibliography.

I have focused on the studio albums of Taylor Swift for this study; however, I will also detail some of her singles as well as some of Swift's television appearances, live recordings, and live and studio videos.

Becoming Fearless

2

THE EARLY YEARS

After demonstrating unusual talent as a singer when she was a child, the daughter of Scott Kingsley Swift and Andrea Gardner Finlay Swift, Taylor, took up the guitar and began writing songs. Because of the fact that Swift's father worked in the field of investments—a field in which relocating the family would not be entirely out of the question—the family was able to move from Pennsylvania to the Nashville area when Swift was 14. In 2005, the 15-year-old Swift became the youngest songwriter signed by the major music publishing company Sony/ATV when she came under contract with Sony/ATV's Tree Music Publishing.[1]

Even before signing her songwriting contract, Swift had received regional and national exposure through concert performances, appearances on the television program *Good Morning America*, and through an Abercrombie & Fitch advertising campaign. As a recording artist, Swift's major nationwide breakthrough came with the release of her debut single, "Tim McGraw." After Swift sent out copies of the record to country disc jockeys asking them to play "Tim McGraw" and after personally promoting the song through social media—via her MySpace page—interest in the recording grew. Eventually, "Tim McGraw" made it into the country Top 10.

This phase of Swift's career found her quickly becoming the leading and most commercially successful singer-songwriter of her generation, at least in part because Taylor Swift was a singing and songwriting prodigy. It found Swift earning not only prestigious awards in the field of country music but also Grammy Awards, thus suggesting that Swift had reached a level of achievement that was highly unusual given her age. In fact, one of the hallmarks of Swift's work as a teenager, especially on her debut album, was the fact that she dealt at times with situations that sounded as though they could have come from the life experiences of someone well beyond Swift's actual age.

TAYLOR SWIFT

Following on the heels of the commercial success of the single release of "Tim McGraw," Big Machine Records released Taylor Swift's self-titled debut album in October 2006. In addition to the earlier hit single, the album generated several other hits that enjoyed a presence on several singles charts, including "Teardrops on My Guitar," "Our Song," "Should've Said No," and "Picture to Burn." The album itself topped the country charts and made it solidly into the Top 10 of the more mainstream pop charts. Interestingly, *Taylor Swift* has continued to enjoy a strong chart presence, seemingly reappearing every time that Swift has released a subsequent album.

The album opens with "Tim McGraw," a collaborative effort of Swift and Liz Rose. Ironically, Rose, who teamed with Swift for songs on Swift's early albums, did not take up songwriting until she was over twice Swift's age when Swift became a professional songwriter. Despite a pairing that might seem unlikely, particularly when so many of Swift's early songs revolved around romantic and other situations that came out of the rural American high school experience, Swift and Rose's songs resonated with the public.

"Tim McGraw" is a song that shares connections on several levels with other bittersweet songs of loss in love. Swift's character tells a boy whom she used to date—via a letter that she never sent—that whenever he thinks of country singer-songwriter Tim McGraw, the singer of the favorite song of Swift's character, she hopes he thinks of her. The bittersweet reflection on a past love seems at least thematically to be related to "Your Wildest Dreams," a Top 10 hit for the Moody Blues, three years before Taylor Swift was born. More immediately with regard to tempo, style, and genre, "Tim McGraw" invites comparisons with Dolly Parton's even earlier hit "I Will Always Love You," a song that made the singles charts for Parton in both the 1970s and 1980s, and which was a massive hit for Whitney Houston in the 1990s and just after Houston's death in the 2010s. Like the chorus section of the Parton composition, "Tim McGraw" makes heavy use of the I–vi–IV–V chord progression (G major, E minor, C major, D major, in the key of G). In fact, this chord progression pervades the Swift song. The progression, widely known as the "oldies progression," dates back to the 1930s and Hoagy Carmichael's composition "Heart and Soul." The progression became a staple of late 1950s and early 1960s street corner doo-wop music and rock-and-roll songs. Swift's heavy use of the progression in "Tim McGraw" gives the song a nostalgic, almost timeless feel. To put it another way, what worked for Hoagy

Carmichael in the 1930s, Dion and the Belmonts in 1961 ("Runaround Sue"), and Dolly Parton in the 1970s works for cowriters Swift and Rose in the 2000s.

The connections between "Tim McGraw" and "I Will Always Love You" run deeper than just a harmonic focus on the oldies progression. Swift's song revolves around a relationship that had ended perhaps a couple of years before the time frame of the song's narrative; Parton's revolves around a relationship that is about to end, because Parton's character senses that she is holding back her partner. Despite the fact that one song looks at a past loss in love and the other looks at an impending breakup, there is clearly the sense of continuing love. Both songs, too, share a sense of the bittersweet as well as a sense of the nostalgic: Swift's a true nostalgia for the past, and Parton's a sense that the characters will, at some time in the future, look back at their relationship with nostalgic eyes.

"Tim McGraw" in no small part defines several aspects of the Taylor Swift melodic style that continues to help define her work over a decade after the song's release. In particular, the song's chorus is motivically based, and each one of the short melodic motives—or figures—is built within a small pitch range. The narrow pitch range and the fact that the chorus tune is built on repetitions of the initial short figure, presentations of the figure starting on different pitches, and manipulations and variations of the figure give the chorus an easy-to-sing quality—it practically invites singing along. To put it another way, the chorus of "Tim McGraw" and its singable engaging nature is one of the work's strongest musical hooks. Others of Swift's major hit songs also tend to owe at least part of their popularity to sing-along friendly chorus tunes, her antibullying song "Mean" being a particularly strong example.

Swift's use of rhythm in the melody of "Tim McGraw" is also notable and is a harbinger of Swift's later work. Particularly in the chorus—but to a certain extent in the verses—Swift makes extensive use of syncopation at the sixteenth-note level. Not only does this lend the melodic rhythm a feeling of energy that might not be entirely expected in a slow ballad such as this song, but it also provides at least a hint of connection to how melodic rhythm is used in such decidedly noncountry genres as alternative rock and hip-hop.

The other aspect of the album's opening track that needs to be considered is the country singer-songwriter Tim McGraw, whose name the song bears. Suffice it to say that McGraw was one of the leading country artists of the 1990s and early 2000s. In fact, arguably some of McGraw's more noteworthy work dated from the early 21st century, including his 2004 album *Live like You Were Dying* and his duet with the hip-hop star Nelly, "Over and Over." Swift's song suggests that the Tim McGraw song that was a favorite of her character and her boyfriend might have dated from just before this period (her character wrote the unsent letter "three summers back"). Even before *Live like You Were Dying*, Tim McGraw was one of the best-known artists in country music; therefore, it is entirely believable that a character such as the one that Swift portrays in her song could have had a McGraw song as her favorite. Interestingly, the success of McGraw's *Live like You Were Dying* and his collaboration with Nelly might have made McGraw seem even more relevant to country fans of Swift's generation than he had been before. McGraw's work since the time of the alleged "letter left unsent" kept McGraw in the public spotlight to an even greater extent than his previous work. As a result, Swift's request that whenever her former lover "think[s] Tim McGraw," he thinks of her, suggests that he will probably be thinking of her quite frequently. He will, in all likelihood, think of her as often as Swift's character thinks of him.

Because Taylor Swift's lyrical focus on her sophomore album, *Fearless*, would move in the direction of her vision of the life of high school students, particularly those who might be considered outsiders, it is interesting to note that "Tim McGraw" and other songs on her debut album are more general and vague about the age of the characters. In addition, it should be noted that although *Fearless* included what would become an iconic juxtaposition of Swift's character (who wears "blue jeans") and her rival (who wears "short skirts" to attract a boy's attention), in "Tim McGraw" Swift's character is at once down home and not necessarily dressed provocatively ("my old faded blue jeans") and sexier and possibly more stereotypically alluring (she also wears a "little black dress").

Study of the lyrics of "Tim McGraw" and the other songs on *Taylor Swift* reveals what came to be part of the Swift modus operandi: the use of capital letters imbedded in the lyrics that apparently reveal secret messages and the identity of the one-time boyfriends who provided the inspiration for the breakup songs. In the album's second track, "Picture to Burn," for example, the text is printed entirely in lowercase letters, except for the letters *D, A, T, E, N, I, C, E, B, O, Y, S*, which are presented over the course of the opening verses and chorus. The lyrics of the song suggest that the fellow whose picture Swift's character wants to burn was not a particularly "nice" boy, thus the message contained in the capitalized letters—*date nice boys*—provides an extension of the message that is contained in the sung lyrics of the song.

This procedure seems interesting, particularly on this album and on *Fearless*. At times, however, as Swift's career has progressed, it can seem as though her calling out of former boyfriends reaches the sort of meanness against which she rails in some of other songs (e.g., "Mean"). So, it seems that some Swift fans might delight in the autobiographical detail—or at least the autobiographical suggestions—that the use of imbedded capital letters provides, while some might find it to be something of a gimmick. What really cannot be denied is that it lends Swift's CD releases added value beyond the actual musical tracks themselves. In fact, Swift's acknowledgments and notes, the way in which the lyrics are presented, the photographs of Swift, and the almost-sensory-overload approach to the use of color and design in the book-let for *Taylor Swift* established a pattern that Swift and her associates at Big

Machine Records have used on every subsequent Swift album to date. In addition to those features, subsequent special editions of *Taylor Swift* have also included extras such as the music videos for "Tim McGraw" and "Teardrops on My Guitar." Sales statistics seem to suggest that the approach continued to be effective, at least into the middle of the second decade of the 21st century. Articles in *Billboard* magazine in 2010 and 2014 noted that Swift's album releases bucked the trend toward the digital download as the purchase vehicle of choice of young consumers.[2] In terms of the CD release as a value-added package, Swift's 2014 album *1989* (named for the year of her birth) goes farther than any of her previous albums; however, Swift's debut clearly established her focus and Big Machine Records' focus on the compact disc medium as a value-added package.

The actual sung lyrics of "Picture to Burn," a Swift-Rose collaboration, suggest that the song's inspiration could be the same boy as the person who inspired "Tim McGraw." The male character in "Tim McGraw" drives a pickup truck that tends to get "stuck on back roads at night," presumably so that the male character can park with Swift's character; the male character of "Picture to Burn" drives a "stupid old pickup truck" that he will not allow Swift's character to drive.

As was the case with "Tim McGraw," there is nothing about the breakup theme or the musical setting that would necessarily be considered cutting edge. However, also like the album's opener, "Picture to Burn" features an engaging and memorable chorus. In fact, it can be argued that even in her earliest work—and whether writing on her own or collaborating with cowriters such as Liz Rose—Taylor Swift's songs tended to contain memorable melodic and lyrical hooks that held up well in comparison to the best pop songs of the time.

On this song, Swift—as she had done on "Tim McGraw"—uses a significant amount of syncopation on the sixteenth-note level in the vocal melody. Interestingly, earlier Southern rock bands, such as Lynyrd Skynyrd, had featured syncopation on this level in their songs from the 1970s. Unlike country (or country rock) predecessors, Swift's use of syncopation is most noticeable in the lead vocal line in the verses. Here, her approach to rhythm exhibits the kind of jazz-influenced flexibility that one can hear in the late 1970s work of Rickie Lee Jones, the early 1970s work of Carole King during her jazziest period (e.g., the 1972 album *Rhymes & Reasons*), and the work of Joni Mitchell throughout the 1970s.

Based on the production style on *Taylor Swift*, it seems that producer Nathan Chapman is owed a huge debt of gratitude in defining the Taylor Swift sound, particularly on the more aggressive songs such as "Picture to Burn." The dense, compressed electric guitar–based texture suggests modern rock of the era; however, it is easy to hear Rob Hajacos's contribution on fiddle and Jeff Hyde's contribution on banjo on the track. In fact, Chapman's electric guitar and Hyde's banjo split the song's instrumental break, thus symbolically tying "Picture to Burn" to the worlds of modern rock and country.

And, despite the country-based references of the lyrics, Swift's syncopated rhythmic style in the verses lean more in the direction of alternative rock than in the direction of country, as had been the case in the ballad "Tim McGraw." This attribute of Swift's melodic style, though, is more noticeable in "Picture to Burn" because of the tempo of the song.

The album's third track and another Swift-Rose collaboration, "Teardrops on My Guitar," continues the stream of memorable lyrical and music hooks. In fact, the very association of Drew, the former boyfriend of Swift's character, with the reason for the "teardrops on [her] guitar" might be one of the more memorable lyrical images on the album. Although her commentary on Taylor Swift's importance as a country-pop-rock singer-songwriter "who makes the whole world sing" was written in 2010, Fleetwood Mac member Stevie Nicks pointed out that Swift's songs are as filled with strong pop hooks as the songs of Neil Diamond and Elton John.[3] Such is the case with "Teardrops on My Guitar." Interestingly, though, the CD edition of *Taylor Swift* contains—as a bonus track—the "pop" version of "Teardrops on My Guitar." Unfortunately, this version of the track significantly de-emphasizes the country ties of the song, particularly in the instrumental accompaniment. The result is a rather anonymous pop ballad. In fact, it might be argued that this mix suggested that—even at the time of the 16-year-old singer-songwriter's debut—a significant reason for the success of her work as a recording artist was that it fell into a hybrid genre that retained clear links to country, rock, and pop. The de-emphasis of the components made the whole of the "pop" mix of "Teardrops on My Guitar" anonymous, and therefore something that could have come from virtually any female pop singer of the time period. The comparison of the two mixes of the song suggests the extent to which the arrangement, the mix, and the production of songs play a significant role in the song's effectiveness. As Taylor Swift continued to mature, it is interesting to note that her songs became easier for artists to adapt to contrasting styles—such as Ryan Adams's singer-songwriter ballad style interpretation of Swift's 2014 pop dance–style song "Shake It Off." At the time of her debut, however, the musical arrangement seemed in no small part to define the song.

The album's next track, "A Place in This World," finds Swift's character trying to find her place in the world. It is a song not only of searching but also of resolve. Thematically and melodically some listeners familiar with popular music of the 1980s might detect connections between "A Place in This World" and "Flashdance ... What a Feeling," the huge Irene Cara hit from the 1983 movie *Flashdance*. Although the theme of empowerment in the face of bullying, being a young social outsider, and being jilted by cheating boyfriends was much more fully developed by Swift on her albums *Fearless* and *Speak Now*, one can hear the roots of the theme in the present song. Interestingly, however, this song does not sound as personal as the best tracks on the album, and it is the only track on *Taylor Swift* in which Swift collaborated with songwriters Robert Ellis Orrall and Angelo Petraglia.

Certainly, neither Taylor Swift nor her early collaborator Liz Rose invented the clever turn of the phrase; however, one of the more memorable images that emerges from Taylor Swift can be found in the song "Cold as You." Here, she tells her former lover that she "has never been anywhere cold as you." The gist of the problem with the relationship, though, is that Swift's character's lover does not appreciate her. She is "not what [he] wanted," and instead of reciprocating her love, he "put[s] up walls and paints them all a shade of gray."

The slow ballad setting of "Cold as You" and Swift's restrained performance of the verses align with the lyrical portrayal of her lover as emotionally disassociated from her. In fact, it might be argued that one of the more interesting aspects of Swift's debut album is that it is at once a very songwriterly collection (for want of a better description) and a showplace for Swift to demonstrate an emotional range as a singer beyond her years. The writerly aspect of the work comes from the fact that the songs make precious few references to the characters' ages, and, in some songs, few references to the exact circumstances that led to difficulty within the relationship. As a result, a song such as "Cold as You," which seems to be about a long-term relationship and possibly a marriage, seems to be something that songsmith Taylor Swift might have written to shop around to established singers. She was, after all, initially signed as a songwriter. What makes the song particularly significant is that Swift manages to pull off the emotional expression of this song, which stands in sharp relief to the assertive and agitated nature of her singing style in a song such as "Picture to Burn."

The writing of the next song, "The Outside," was credited solely to Swift. Although this piece might not be as well remembered as "Picture to Burn" or "Tim McGraw," "The Outside" was quite popular at the time of the album's release. In fact, *People* magazine included the song on its list of essential digital downloads for the second week of November 2006.[4]

Musically, "The Outside" is typical of Swift's early approach: there is significant syncopation in the melody, the rhythm of the melody also alternates between phrases that primarily feature syncopation on the eighth-note (half-beat) level and those that feature rhythmic activity and syncopation on the sixteenth-note (quarter-beat) level, the melody of the verses is primarily based on short motives, and the chorus tune provides a memorable commercial hook. Also particularly interesting is the way in which the melody in the first half of the chorus is constructed. It is particularly fascinating to listen to the alternation between registers and how the lower-range figures relate to each other and start on successively lower notes. This gives the first half of the chorus a feeling of being a thought-out whole. The contrast between this and the freer-ranging second half of the chorus seems to align with the sentiments of alienation that Swift expresses in her lyrics. As is the case with other fast songs on the album, the sixteenth-note level syncopation in "The Outside" suggests a connection with alternative rock as well as with the 1970s jazz-influenced work of Carole King, Joni Mitchell, and Ricky Lee Jones mentioned earlier.

Like so many of the songs that have been associated with Taylor Swift over the years, "The Outside" can be interpreted as a breakup song. In contrast to some of her more pointed works—particularly the songs that fans and critics have interpreted as being directed at specific high-profile past boyfriends—"The Outside" is more metaphorical. In fact, the alienation that Swift's character feels in her relationship does not necessarily have to be interpreted as that of a romantic relationship. Here, the lyrics are left vague enough that Swift's character can be understood as standing on "the outside looking in" on a close friendship in which she and the character she addresses have grown increasingly distant, and now apparently irreconcilably so. I would argue that a song such as "The Outside" that is open more fully to interpretation than some of the other songs on *Taylor Swift* is more likely to be the kind of Swift composition that is most open to being covered by other performers: the song is commercial, has interesting melodic and rhythmic hooks, and is built around lyrical imagery that somehow seems more mature than that of some of the other songs from early in Swift's songwriting career.

The next track, the Swift-Rose collaboration "Tied Together with a Smile," can seem like something of an outlier on *Taylor Swift* as one listens to the album in sequence. In this song, Swift's character addresses a person who is "tied together with a smile," even though they are "coming undone." It is an acknowledgment that the other character hides behind a smile even though she suffers from feelings of inferiority and low self-esteem. This character is apparently a young woman who relies on sexual promiscuity in order to achieve some sort of feeling of connection to others. Swift's character points out that the other character will never feel whole and will never overcome her feelings of alienation until she learns to love herself. Although it might make the most sense to experience *Taylor Swift* as a collection of individual tracks—the album does not exhibit the same degree of concept album–like cohesion as some of Swift's later work—it is notable that "Tied Together with a Smile" revisits the image of an individual hiding her hurt, pain, and lack of self-esteem behind a smile that one can detect in "Teardrops on My Guitar," in which Swift's character "fake[s] a smile" when talking with her ex-lover as he describes his new love interest.

The verses of "Tied Together with a Smile" are noteworthy for how they break out of conventional structure. The melody of each verse is built in two-measure phrases in an AAABB[1] relationship. In so far as phrases in pop songs tend to be built in units of four or eight measures, it is unusual for a verse section to be ten measures in length. But it is not the sheer number of measures that is unusual about the phrase structure in the verses: the last two-measure unit (B[1]) also seems to stand somewhat alone, because in it the lyrics offer a commentary on the sentiments of the previous eight measures. This is an example of the kind of structural anomaly that is not entirely outside the realm of possibility in folk music–inspired country music. In fact, "Tied Together with a Smile" stands out on this album as possibly the most overtly "country sounding" song in the collection, in part because of the phrase structure, but also because of the prominence of acoustic guitar, fiddle, and Dobro in the accompaniment texture. It should be noted that this is the kind of structural phenomenon that one might resist as a writer if one were to move in the direction of more conventional pop or dance club music. To put it another way, this kind of musical construction would become less likely for Swift to pursue on albums such as *Red* and *1989*.

"Stay Beautiful," another collaborative effort of Swift and Liz Rose, concerns a character named Cory, whom Swift's character admires from afar, as do all of "the pretty girls on every corner." The gist of the song seems to be that Cory does not realize just how attractive he is. Apparently, he does not recognize Swift's character's desire for him. Although the specifics of the situation differ from those of the album's other songs, "Stay Beautiful" continues the general theme of unrequited love that weaves throughout the album. Incidentally, Swift's coded message in the CD booklet for "Stay Beautiful" is "SHAKE N BAKE." Although urban slang of the day includes a number of possible meanings of the phrase, including a low-budget portable lab for making crystal methamphetamine and smoking marijuana outside in the cold, the "hidden" phrase here seems to refer to the intensity of Cory's appeal to Swift's character.

The musical setting of "Stay Beautiful" is notable for the tunefulness of the chorus, although that trait runs throughout Swift's collaborative and solo compositions on this album. The listener may detect at least a bit of a connection between the chorus of this song and that of "Tim McGraw" because of the extensive use of the I–vi–IV–V "oldies" progression. Incidentally, Taylor Swift's use of this tried and true progression is not limited to these two songs on her debut album: she also used the progression extensively on "The Best Day," a track from her 2008 album *Fearless*.

In the printed lyrics of "Should've Said No" in the CD's booklet, Swift coded the name of the boy who inspired the song. In fact, Swift's modus operandi of delivering coded messages was and continued to be pretty obvious; it did not take much thought by a music consumer to figure out what was up with the unexpected mixtures of lowercase and capital letters in the presentation of the lyrics in the CD booklet. And, in fact, Swift almost seemed at times to go out her way to let her fans know exactly what she was doing in these "coded" messages. For example, in an early interview with Brian Mansfield for *USA Today*, Swift readily acknowledged that the booklet's lyrics for "Should've Said No" contained the name of the boy who inspired the song coded into the lyrics.[5] For those interested in the autobiographical details of Swift's songs, the young man's name was "Sam," based on the capital letters in the text. The lyrics find Swift's character telling Sam that he "should've said no" when he had the opportunity to cheat on Swift with another girl. Swift tells him that if he had done so, he might still have her and not find himself crawling back "on [his] knees" begging for forgiveness. The strength of the instrumental arrangement and production and passion of Swift's singing style suggest empowerment—her character is clearly in charge of the situation.

"Should've Said No" is one of the few songs on the album credited solely to Swift. It is worth noting that there are few, if any, clear differences between the musical materials and styles or the lyrical focal points or techniques of "Should've Said No, "Our Song," and "The Outside," the solo compositions, and those found in the collaborative works. The three solo compositions run across a fairly wide stylistic gamut; however, that is true of the other songs as well. "Should've Said No" exhibits a bit of the texture of the classic rock power ballad as a result of guitarist-producer Nathan Chapman's electric guitar tone and his production style on the track. Interestingly, the instrumental introduction and the similar instrumental break section later in the sound suggest a modern take on the genre of the traditional fiddle tune. The use of the fiddle alongside multiple unison instruments playing the figure in part suggests the influence of old Anglo-American fiddle tunes; however, the possible influence of traditional folk music is reinforced by the emphasis on minor chords and the predominance of the pentatonic scale (frequently used in traditional Anglo-American folk music) in the instrumental figure.

"Mary's Song (Oh My My My)," a collaborative composition of Swift, Liz Rose, and Brian Maher, stands apart from the bulk of Taylor Swift's early work in that it is a third-person observational song, presumably from the viewpoint of the Mary of the song's title. This is a rarity among Swift's early work, too, in that it is a song about a relationship that has been through its trials and tribulations, but that ultimately survives and finds both members of the couple anticipating growing old together. Swift drives the point of the song home in the coded message contained in the capital letters in the CD booklet's presentation of the lyrics: "Sometimes love is forever." In part because the lyrics are not autobiographical or autobiographical-sounding (given the third-person nature of the text) and in part because the musical setting has a fairly traditional folk-country flavor to it, "Mary's Song (Oh My My My)" seems like an ideal Taylor Swift contender to be covered by any number of country artists. In fact, it might strike some listeners as the kind of song that one might write as a contract songwriter. It is engaging and contains a lyrical premise and music that are likely to appeal to a wide country listenership.

"Our Song," a solo composition by Swift, concluded the original release of the album. The gist of the lyrics is that Swift's character is riding in a car with her boyfriend. As they listen to the radio, Swift's character realizes that they have not laid claim to "our song" and mentions the fact. Her boyfriend counters that their song consists of all of the sounds that he associates with their relationship. Interestingly, this piece exhibits some connections to some of the other songs on the album, despite the fact that the lyrical theme deviates from that of many of the other songs. For one thing, the brief instrumental break figures in "Our Song" resemble the lengthier, apparently fiddle-tune-inspired breaks in "Should've Said No." For another, the chorus places significant emphasis on the fifth scale-step, something that happens on several other tracks. Similar to other songs, but certainly not to the degree that Swift uses on "Picture to Burn," the verses have a conversational quality, which is achieved by a relatively high number of repeated pitches in the lower register of Swift's voice. This gives the impression of a heightened speech and makes the chorus stand in sharp contrast to the more obviously tuneful, higher-pitched, and wider-ranging melody of the chorus.

Between 2006 and 2008, Big Machine Records issued several new editions of *Taylor Swift*, each of which included various bonus audio tracks and music videos. For example, the 2008 enhanced edition (Big Machine Records CMR079102) included the tracks "I'm Only Me When I'm with You," "Invisible," "Perfectly Good Heart," and the pop mix of "Teardrops on My Guitar" as well as the music videos for "Tim McGraw" and "Teardrops on My Guitar." Because the bonus tracks have been widely associated with the album ever since 2008, let us examine the three songs that were not present on the original album.

"I'm Only Me When I'm with You" is a product of the same songwriting team that penned "A Place in This World" (Swift, Robert Ellis Orrall, and Angelo Petraglia). Although she is not yet 30 years old at the time of this writing, it has been interesting to observe the changes in Taylor Swift as a songwriter. Among singer-songwriters, she is unusual in getting such an early start. Consider, for example, John Lennon, whose first commercially successful songs were written when he was a half-decade older than Swift when she wrote her first hit. Even among former young prodigy country singer-songwriters, such as Dolly Parton, Swift was younger when she enjoyed her first hits. Therefore, it perhaps is not surprising that her maturation as a young woman has played out in songs to a greater extent than what typically would be the case with singer-songwriters whose careers begin beyond their teen-aged years. Germane to this particular song is the fact that Swift's character can be understood as fully tying her own identity to that of her boyfriend. The characters that would populate her next albums generally were less inclined to do so. In fact, as Swift's characters defined themselves based less on their love interests, they grew in their expressions of empowerment. To put it another way, the empowerment of "Picture to Burn" and "Should've Said No" became a more consistent theme as Swift matured as a writer and made the sentiments of songs such as "I'm Only Me When I'm with You" seem more like those associated with fictional characters and not with Swift.

Although "I'm Only Me When I'm with You" is an engaging song from the musical standpoint, it does not sound entirely novel in the context of the album. Some of the melodic phrases of the verses closely resemble those of Swift's first hit, "Tim McGraw." This—and the fact that it finds Swift's character so fully associating her self-identity with her boyfriend—may explain the fact that "I'm Only Me When I'm with You" was relegated to the status of bonus track on the 2008 enhanced edition of *Taylor Swift*.

Swift collaborated with Robert Orrall in writing the next bonus track, "Invisible." The text basically sums up the plight of Swift's characters that run throughout the original, official version of the album. Here, her character is in love with a boy to whom she is "invisible." Although her character's condition is expressed in different ways with respect to the details, this lack of recognition of love is at the root of such songs as "Stay Beautiful," in which Cory does not recognize the affection that Swift's character and the "other girls on the street" have for him, and "Teardrops on My Guitar," in which Drew does not recognize the pain that he causes for Swift's character when he mentions "that [other] girl that he talks about." In fact, it can be argued that *Taylor Swift* is largely about alienation in the romantic sphere of life. Interestingly, although romance/love runs through Swift's sophomore album, *Fearless*, the alienation felt by her characters broadens into various aspects of high school life. Specifically, she portrays the social outsider. As Swift continued to mature as a writer through *Fearless* into her 2010 album *Speak Now*, she increasingly portrayed empowered women who stood up to those—boyfriends or others—who tried to alienate them from the world around them.

"A Perfectly Good Heart," composed by Swift, Brett James, and Troy Verges, concludes the 2008 special edition version of the album. This is another song of heartbreak, in which Swift's character—as had been the case throughout the album—has her heart broken by a boy. The piece is fairly conventional in its lyrics and musical setting, particularly considering how immediately engaging some of the lyrical twists and some of the musical hooks of the album's official songs are. In fact, it can be argued that this is an example of the kind of work that a professional songwriter would produce to provide as a potential single or album track for any number of artists. As Swift continued to progress as a performing talent over the course of her next several albums, I would argue that some of her best work can be found in the less conventional songs, and especially in the songs in which she writes and sings a more conversational-style, almost jazz-influenced verse. It is not that there is anything necessarily wrong with "A Perfectly Good Heart," but it comes off as somewhat generic compared with the best of the songs that actually made the original running order of *Taylor Swift*.

By the time of Swift's next album, *Fearless*, her work would receive considerably more attention from music critics. *Fearless* and subsequent albums also tended to receive positive reaction from the critics. Critical reaction to *Taylor Swift* might best be summed up by Ralph Novak's review in *People*. Although generally positive, the review expresses some apprehension about the depth of Swift's talent and refers to her as "Nashville's answer to Brittany Spears."[6] Although some critics seemed to fixate on the teen-girlish side of Swift's singing, other critics praised Swift's ability to use familiar songwriting techniques in ways that sounded original and novel. For example, All Music Guide's Jeff Tamarkin wrote the "device" of "associated a failed affair with items, places, and people" of the song "Tim McGraw" had been used by countless songwriters, but here managed to sound like "an original idea."[7] Likewise, Tamarkin praised the "sophisticated" maturity of Swift's lyrics in "Cold as You."

Although Taylor Swift seemed to come out of nowhere into the music industry—she was only 16 at the time of her debut album—the album and its singles performed well on the sales charts. The album itself topped the country charts and enjoyed a solid performance on the pop album charts as well, making it into the middle of the Top 10. Interestingly, as Taylor Swift subsequently became an even bigger star, her debut album returned to the charts, appearing again in 2010, 2012, 2013, and 2014, roughly corresponding to the release dates of Swift's subsequent albums *Red*, *Speak Now*, and *1989*, albums that increasingly found Swift moving from the country genre to more mainstream pop.

Interestingly, after the release of the album, singles drawn from it made strong performances on the country and pop charts through 2008 and the release of Swift's second album, *Fearless*. "Teardrops on My Guitar" reached No. 2 on *Billboard* magazine's country charts and No. 11 on the pop charts; "Our Song" was a No. 1 country hit and peaked at No. 16 on the *Billboard* Hot 100; in 2008, "You Should've Said No" reached No. 1 on the country charts, and "Picture to Burn" reached No. 3 on the country charts.[8]

In the wake of her initial success, Swift partnered with Target Corporation for an exclusive in-store release of a 2007 Christmas EP (extended play) called *The Taylor Swift Holiday Collection*. The disc included the tracks "Last Christmas," "Christmases When You Were Mine," "Santa Baby," "Silent Night," "Christmas Must Be Something More," and "White Christmas." After the EP's initial run in Target stores, it was more widely released as a CD and for digital download.

The EP opens with George Michael's composition "Last Christmas," which originally had been a 1984 hit for Michael's pop duo, Wham! Arguably, this is the most successful cover on *The Taylor Swift Holiday Collection*. Michael's song uses an unconventional phrase structure and is text-heavy, two of the attributes of some of Swift's more successful early songs. "Last Christmas" also lends itself to Swift's vocal style, particularly with respect to her interpretation of rhythmic syncopation. To put it another way, if one were to pick the ideal, most Swift-like holiday song for Swift to cover, this probably would be the most logical choice.

The EP's second track, Swift, Nathan Chapman, and Liz Rose's "Christmases When You Were Mine," is in a classic Tin Pan Alley–style AABA form, something of a rarity in the Taylor Swift canon. The tune, harmony, and acoustic guitar–based accompaniment all have a "classic" feel, too. In fact, the acoustic nature of the song might call to mind predecessors such as Paul McCartney's "Blackbird" or some of the early songs of James Taylor. In typically Taylor Swift style, however, the piece is dense with lyrics that exhibit at least a bit of an improvisatory feel. Perhaps most notable, however, is the catchy melody of the A sections. The tunes start on the third scale-step, move upward through a wide range, and then descend to scale-step 5, which is more dramatic in range than a typical Swift verse tune in one of her country, pop, or rock songs; however, it is instantly recognizable and memorable, like the best of her work.

Swift's performance of the early 1950s song "Santa Baby" is not as stylized (one might reasonably say not as quirky or even overacted) as Madonna's 1987 Marilyn Monroe–influenced version. In fact, the coy sexuality of Eartha Kitt's original version and Madonna's version is largely absent in Swift's interpretation. This, instead, is a fairly straightforward country version, featuring an instrumentation and arrangement that sounds as though it comes directly out of Swift and producer Nathan Chapman's work on Swift's debut album.

The inclusion of "Silent Night" on the EP is curious in that Swift's version uses the traditional English translation of Joseph Mohr's poem "Stille Nacht," but with Swift's original music. It could be a function of the fact that the lines of the lyrics are so short, especially compared with Swift's lyrics in her wide-ranging songs of the period, such as the well-known hits "Tim McGraw" and "Picture to Burn," or a function of reverence, but Swift's musical setting is absent the syncopation and the perky motivic nature of her most memorable early hit songs. These were some of the attributes of Swift's early compositions that also played to her strengths as a singer. For a young songwriter, creating a new setting of Mohr's text would seem to be a situation in which there would be little chance for a win; so ingrained, so popular, and so distinctive is Franz Gruber's original tune and simple harmonization.

Swift contributed one solo composition to the EP: "Christmas Must Be Something More." In this up-tempo, contemporary country–style song, Swift contrasts the superficial aspects of Christmas (e.g., kissing under mistletoe, ribbons, gift boxes, snow) with the true meaning of Christmas as a Christian holiday. Although Swift sings that the holiday is "something holy; not superficial," her proclamation, "here's to the birthday boy who saved our lives," might be heard by some listeners as simply too irreverent. To put it another way, the "birthday boy" reference is the kind of turn of phrase that probably guarantees that "Christmas Must Be Something More" will never become a Contemporary Christian classic. Interestingly, in the final statement of the chorus, Swift changes "the birthday boy" to "Jesus Christ." From a musical standpoint, it is worth comparing Swift's use of melody in this song to her use of melody in a song such as "Teardrops on My Guitar." In both songs, the main part of the melody rides in a part of Swift's vocal range in which she sounds perhaps at her most comfortable. In these songs, and in her other (for want of a better word) natural-sounding compositions from approximately 2006–2008, Swift the songwriter clearly played to the strengths of Swift the singer.

Swift and her accompanying instrumentalists, led by Nathan Chapman, give Irving Berlin's standard "White Christmas" (reputed to be one of the, if not the, most recorded song in the history of sound recording) a distinctively country-style reading. Interestingly, the instrumental introduction, which is reprised at the track's conclusion, bears more than a passing resemblance to the instrumental texture of Swift's first hit, "Tim McGraw." The instrumentation of "White Christmas," with its emphasis on acoustic guitar, mandolin, fiddle, and Dobro, also resembles the arrangement on "Tim McGraw." This is an interpretation of "White Christmas" that stands apart from many others. The connections of the arrangement and performance to "Tim McGraw" also clearly put the "Taylor Swift" stamp on Berlin's classic tune.

All in all, *The Taylor Swift Holiday Collection* is an uneven EP. It tends to bear the mark of a collection that was put together to take advantage of Swift's early, perhaps unexpected, success as a singer-songwriter. One might imagine that had her first Christmas collection been produced for 2008, 2009, or even a later release (e.g., after *Fearless* made Swift a superstar), the album or EP would have been more consistent in playing to Swift's strengths as a performer.

Big Machine Records released another Taylor Swift EP disc, *Beautiful Eyes*, in Wal-Mart stores in 2008. In addition to Swift songs that appeared on her self-titled debut (e.g., "Picture to Burn," "Teardrops on My Guitar," "Should've Said No"), *Beautiful Eyes* contained two songs not released on any official Swift album: "Beautiful Eyes" and "I Heart ?" The EP's title track bears some musical resemblance—particularly in the melodic shapes just before the chorus—to "Teardrops on My Guitar." Swift's use of the fragment "I don't know why" also calls to mind "Teardrops on My Guitar," as she uses the line in both songs. In "Teardrops on My Guitar," Swift uses a similar line in response to her observation that her former lover, Drew, is "the song in the car I keep singing." In "Beautiful Eyes," Swift uses the line in reference to the reason that "I think of you [her new love interest] late at night." Unlike the bulk of Swift's early material, "Beautiful Eyes" suggests the promise of love, as opposed to the loss of love. Rhetorically, it is as though this song precedes the experiences that Swift shares throughout her debut album. Despite some stylistic ties in the melody and in the musical arrangement to songs such as "Teardrops on My Guitar," "Beautiful Eyes" is marked by the use of suspended (added note) chords that help to create a lush harmonic background.

Although the title of the EP's other new track, "I Heart?," might call to mind hip-hop song titles or even old 1980s Prince titles such as "I Would Die 4 U," this song thoroughly represents Swift's approach to country music. The song is also notable for Swift's patter-like, improvised-sounding approach in the verses, a trait found in some of the more effective songs on her first several albums and a trait that suggests the possible influence of her jazz-inspired predecessors, such as Joni Mitchell and Ricky Lee Jones, as well as Carole King's work on *Rhymes & Reasons*. This seems like a song with strong commercial potential; however, the fact that Swift's debut album contained similar songs, and that "I Heart ?" was not more widely distributed, suggests that it was not quite up to the standards of a long-lasting major hit such as "Picture to Burn."

FEARLESS[9]

Perhaps the biggest surprise of the period 2008–2010 in the music industry was the tremendous success of 18-year-old Taylor Swift's second album, *Fearless*. The album won multiple American music awards, numerous country music–related awards, a Grammy for Best Country Album, and a Grammy for Album of the Year, among other critical accolades. Perhaps best remembered (and unfortunately so), however, was rapper Kanye West's interruption of Swift's acceptance speech for Best Female Video (for "You Belong with Me") at MTV's Video Music Awards show.[10] The album went multiplatinum and topped the country and pop charts. All of the awards and sale and chart statistics, though, do not get at the heart of the importance of *Fearless*: it is essentially a concept album about overcoming obstacles, ostensibly written about the experiences of teenagers but reflecting an unusual maturity combined with strong commercial musical appeal. And all of the songs were either written or cowritten by the 18-year-old Swift. Interestingly, although most of the songs on Swift's debut album provided little direct reference to the age of the characters, the focus of *Fearless* is clearly on Swift's view of what American teenagers go through during their high school years. In fact, this focus is clearly emphasized by the CD booklet's photographs and its visual production style.

The album opens with its title track, a song in which Swift's character ultimately shares the first kiss with a young man who sweeps her off her feet. This product of Swift, Liz Rose, and Hillary Lindsey is not the most profound song ever written; however, it captures the spirit of a moment experienced by many people. And that is a major point of the album: it contains songs that address experiences shared by the masses, even if they are experiences between just two individuals. These experiences are set to music that is as universal as possible. For example, in "Fearless" one can hear hints of country, pop, folk, and even alternative rock. Once the listener goes beneath the surface, "Fearless" and other tracks on the album are notable for their subtle mix of unexpected musical influences in the drumbeats, guitar parts, other instrumental tone colors, and so on.

In "Fifteen," a song that Swift penned alone, she addresses a 15-year-old girl with the voice of experience. The basic message reflects the old saying "If I knew then what I know now . . . ." Swift's character tells the girl about her high school experiences with her best friend and about her friend losing her virginity to a boy who "changed his mind" about long-term commitment. Her warning to "look before you fall" is set to music that can only be described as pop—there is little overt (or stereotypical) reference to country music. The instrumental introduction, interludes, and accompaniment are notable for the harmonic richness of suspended- and added-note chords. This approach to harmony seems to emerge out of Swift's earlier work on the title track from her 2008 *Beautiful Eyes* EP.

Fearless spawned several successful singles; however, the highest charting was "Love Story." In this song, Swift took the familiar Shakespearian story of Romeo and Juliet as a jumping-off point. In Swift's retelling of the story, her character's father is against the relationship, but Swift persists in asking her "Romeo" to "take [her] somewhere where we can be alone." By the end of the song, Swift's lover has talked to her father and asks Swift's character to marry him. Although this brief synopsis might make the song sound formulaic (not to mention less dramatically intense than the storyline in Shakespeare's play), the melodic hooks are strong enough to overcome the predictability of the lyrics. *Fearless* can be thought of as the album that moved Taylor Swift from the status of singer-songwriter prodigy to singer-songwriter superstar. Although the album included several songs that were among the biggest hits of the day, the single release of "Love Story" was without peer: it is reputed to be one of the biggest-selling singles of all time.

Similar to its predecessor, "Hey Stephen" uses generally conventional imagery, but Swift's performance and her melodic writing make the song enjoyable and engaging anyway. In this case, she turns to the image of the handsome boy, the title character, in whom "all the girls" are interested. The girls toss stones at Stephen's window to try to get his attention; however, Swift's character tells Stephen that she is the only "one waiting there even when it's cold." In a slight turn from what the listener might anticipate, Swift makes her case for Stephen to choose her over the others by singing "they're beautiful, but would they write a song for you?" In asking this question, Swift aligns herself, albeit in a small way, with the tradition of American singer-songwriters going back to the 1970s—that is, singer-songwriters who write autobiographical-sounding songs in which they at least mention the fact that they are a songwriter.

Liz Rose collaborated with Swift in writing "White Horse." In this song, Swift portrays a woman who dreamed that her romance would last, only to be let down by her lover. In the chorus, she tells him that "it's too late for you and your white horse" to return to her and to rekindle the relationship. The lyrical imagery is familiar: Taylor Swift refers to her dreams of being "a princess" in both "White Horse" and in "Love Story," and she uses the image of "an angel" in both "White Horse" and "Hey Stephen." Again, it is the performance—the feeling of sadness and resignation that Swift projects as a singer—and the engaging music and musical arrangement that really make the song work effectively.

Throughout *Fearless*, Swift moves between situations and characters that clearly relate to high school age, to those that could be as apropos to college students and 20-somethings. "You Belong with Me" presents a situation right out of American high schools: Swift's character is in love with a boy who has a girlfriend (a cheerleader who "wears short skirts") who seems to be much more desirable than Swift's character (pictured in the liner booklet as a glasses-wearing clarinet player in the pep band), but Swift's character tells the boy, "you belong with me." The situation is not entirely removed from that of "Hey Stephen" except that in "You Belong with Me," the girlfriend emerges as Swift's sole competition. What makes "You Belong with Me" truly interesting as a country pop hybrid is the musical setting. The piece reflects elements of early 1980s new wave rock: most notably, the beat, tempo, and the steady repeated eighth notes in the accompanying instruments. Highly unusual, however, is the fact that at various points in the recording, fiddle, banjo, and mandolin join the steady eighth-note texture.

In the slow ballad "Breathe," Swift portrays the one who ended a relationship. Despite this, her character feels a strong sense of loss (e.g., "I can't breathe without you"). While "Breathe" is not the most memorable track on the album, it is notable for cowriter Colbie Caillat's vocal harmony work. Caillat sings with a tone color that so closely matches Swift's lead that listeners might think that the duet texture is actually Swift double-tracked.

The theme of fearlessness is more difficult to sense in some songs than in others. Clearly, in "Breathe," Swift's character overcame whatever trepidations she had and "drove away" from a relationship. In "Tell Me Why," her character also clearly grapples with her fears. In this Swift/Liz Rose collaboration, Swift's character "took a chance" on a relationship about which she had concerns, and after her lover constantly puts her down and exhibits his "mean streak" and "temper," she ends the relationship. Musically, the piece integrates several intriguing elements to create a hybrid sound with interesting textures. The highly syncopated drumbeat, while not quite the product of 1990s alternative rock or hip-hop, at least moves in that direction. Likewise, the tone color of the electric guitar parts comes more from the world of rock than from the world of country. However, the piece opens with the fiddle, a clear reference to the country music tradition.

In "You're Not Sorry," Swift continues the basic narrative of empowerment in the face of repeated transgressions by her character's lover that she explored in "White Horse" and "Tell Me Why." Perhaps sensing that the theme might be wearing a bit thin, Swift and cowriter John Rich turned in a different direction in "The Way I Loved You." In this piece, Swift's character is locked in a safe, loving, caring, "comfortable" relationship in which her lover seems to be the perfect gentleman, the one who makes "all my single friends ... jealous." The problem is that all of the passion has left her life, because the man with whom she originally fell in love was "wild and crazy." The repressed dissatisfaction of her character, the wide dynamic and textural changes, and the use of distorted electric guitars in the loud sections of the song suggest (strange as it may sound) a country pop take on 1990s grunge.

In "Forever & Always," Swift's character suffers from a different sort of relationship problem. Here, her boyfriend has become distant ("he still hasn't called") despite the fact that at an earlier point in the relationship he had declared that they would be together "forever and always." As is the case with other songs on the album, Swift's singing, the instrumental work, the arrangements, the production, the melodic material, and so on are all pleasant and radio-friendly. One of the problems with Swift's approach is that so many of her songs deal with boyfriend-girlfriend relationships from so many different angles that it is difficult on this album to get a strong sense of who Taylor Swift is. In the world of stand-alone pop songs, this is not really a problem; however, in the post-1970 world of singer-songwriters, when the emphasis has been on introspection, personal confession, and autobiography, Swift's approach on songs such as "Forever & Always" can come across as a bit too generic and market-driven.

The same could not be said for "The Best Day," a song in which Swift sounds thoroughly convincing as an introspective, real emotion-driven singer-songwriter. In this piece, she reflects on her relationship with and perception of her father over the years. The close bond of which Swift sings and the perception of her father as a loving, supportive hero in her life are supported by the acknowledgment that she gives to him in the album's liner notes.[11] Swift's music falls into a nearly Eagles-like easygoing country rock style. The harmonic progression of the verses, I–vi–IV–V, often referred to as the oldies progression, has been a staple of American popular songs since Hoagy Carmichael's "Heart and Soul" in the 1930s. This chord progression was especially prominent in the pop music of the late 1950s. Interestingly, Swift references late 1950s pop in the chorus of "The Best Day" when she articulates the word "fall" as "fa-a-all," in the manner of Buddy Holly. The harmonic material, the Eagles-like style, the introspective sounding vocal approach, and the Holly reference (whether intentional or unintentional), all give "The Best Day" a timeless quality.

Fearless concludes with "Change," a song that opens with dramatic, high-volume, almost fanfare-like distorted electric guitars, electric bass, and drums. As she did in "The Way I Loved You," Swift uses wide dynamic contrasts to add musical definition to the contrasting lyrics of the verses and chorus. In this song, the text of the relatively quiet, laid-back verses deals with life's difficulties metaphorically, while the intense louder chorus offers promise of breaking down the "walls that they put up to hold us back." Swift is deliberately vague enough in her imagery that "Change" can be understood in a variety of ways. For example, given her earlier focus on the in-people and the out-people of high school cliques, "they" could refer to the students who would exclude members of Swift's group. On the other hand, given her earlier focus on boys who have wronged her character and the other female characters of her songs, "they" could be insensitive boys and men. But the song can also be understood on a wider political and social level. It is a promise of overcoming obstacles and oppression.

In the CD's booklet, Taylor Swift provides an explanation of her definition of the word "fearless." All of the songs on the album meet her definition to some extent. Significantly, she and coproducer Nathan Chapman sequenced the tracks so that the album's bookends and several key songs throughout bring the listener back to the theme of fearlessness with clarity. *Fearless* is therefore something of a concept album. It is also, however, something of a collection of individual songs that at times seem to be somewhat at odds with each other—it really depends on the listener's viewpoint. Whether one experiences *Fearless* as a theme-based album or as a collection of disparate tracks, the compositions are engaging, Swift's singing is pleasant, and the arrangements and production are impeccable. It is easy to understand why this was one of the best-selling albums of the first decade of the 21st century. *Fearless* also is indicative of a 21st-century marketing trend in CD recordings: the inclusion of enhanced bonus material, in this case including web links and computer-playable official videos for "Change" and "Love Story," lends the CD release a value-added feel that goes beyond what one might receive if one purchased the album as a download. The platinum edition of the album also includes Swift and rapper T-Pain's hilarious collaborative performance of Swift's rap "Thug Story" (a parody of "Love Story") as well as several behind-the-scenes documentaries about the making of the official videos for the album, including "You Belong with Me," probably the best-known video from *Fearless.*

Critical reaction to *Fearless* was overwhelmingly positive. In addition to the award that Swift won for the video of "You Belong with Me," *Fearless* won Grammy Awards for Best Country Album and Album of the Year. Writing in various magazines and newspapers, a range of music critics touted the album. For example, the title of the brief article, "Buy These Now," suggests *Rolling Stone*'s reaction to *Fearless,*[12] as does the title of Elysa Gardner's review in *USA Today*: "Taylor Swift Hits All the Right Words."[13] Perusal of the "Annotated Bibliography" will reveal several other favorable reviews from the popular press.

Although the focus of this volume is on Taylor Swift's albums, throughout her career, Swift has released significant singles that did not appear on her albums. In most cases, the songs were part of motion-picture soundtracks and as such appeared on the soundtrack albums for those movies, or they were singles that eventually came to be offered as bonus tracks on later editions of Swift's albums. One of the soundtrack singles from this part of Swift's career was the song "Crazier," from *Hannah Montana: The Movie*, which I will discuss in more detail in Chapter 5, "Beyond Music."

It should be noted that some of Taylor Swift's fans were taken at least somewhat by surprise by Swift's move away from country and country rock on later albums such as *Red* (2012) and *1989* (2014). As her first two albums suggested, though, Taylor Swift has never truly been solely a country artist. Perhaps even more to the point in demonstrating Swift's tendency to work in unexpected musical hybridizations was her November 2008 appearance on *CMT Crossroads* in which she performed with the British hard rock band Def Leppard. Big Machine Records released this performance on DVD in 2009. The crossover nature of Swift's compositions is touched on in the video's interview and discussion segment. As several members of Def Leppard put it, if one removes the banjo and fiddle from Taylor Swift's most overtly country-sounding compositions (based on their instrumentation), the songs closely resemble noncountry pop music and are easily adaptable to a wide variety of genres.[14]

This initial phase of Taylor Swift's career, which encompassed her work from approximately ages 16–18, found the young singer-songwriter moving from the status of prodigy to all-out superstar. In particular, the songs of *Fearless*—although focused on life in American high schools—suggested commercial songwriting maturity beyond Swift's years. Swift's early fan base was established in part through the use of social media, at the time primarily a domain for the young; however, Swift's appeal crossed generational lines to a greater extent than most stars of her age. In fact, this continued to be true and was mentioned in some reviews of Swift's recordings.[15]

The "Mean" Era

3

In this second phase of Taylor Swift's career, the award-winning prodigy continued to grow in lyrical maturity. Although country music continued to play a significant role in defining the work of Swift during this time period, Swift ventured away from country and country rock more so than she had done on *Taylor Swift* and *Fearless*. Swift also continued to maintain a strong social media presence. Now, however, instead of using social media to introduce music fans and individuals in the music industry to her work, she used social media to stay in contact with loyal fans. Swift also increasingly was seen as a supporter of empowerment for women, for those who were and are bullied, and in general for social outsiders. Interestingly, Swift's music and public statements of empowerment elicited mixed reactions from members of her generation and from feminists of a previous generation. As had been the case with Swift's first two albums, her work during this phase of her career continued to suggest the possible influence of the confessional singer-songwriters of the early 1970s: Swift's work remained deeply autobiographical.

Speak Now

As Swift describes her 2010 album *Speak Now* in the CD's liner notes, the collection represents "songs [that are] made up of words I didn't say when the moment was right in front of me. These songs are open letters. Each is written with a specific person in mind, telling them what I meant to tell them in person."[1] Swift goes on to invite her audience not to miss the opportunity to share their feelings. She writes, ". . . I think the words you stop yourself from saying are the ones that will haunt you the longest."[2] By sharing her feelings, Swift plays the role of the empowered. In the songs in which she was wronged—by a former lover, by a music critic, by a girl who stole something from her in the playground as a youth, and so on—she stands up for herself in her song lyrics. And, significantly, these are all Swift's lyrics, as well as her music, as *Speak Now* was the first Taylor Swift album on which she did not share at least some songwriting credits with others.

One of the challenges posed by Swift's self-described approach to writing the songs on *Speak Now* is that it does not appear to be all that different from the diary-like approach that she used at least in some of the songs on her previous two albums, perhaps most clearly on *Taylor Swift*. Based on the situations that one can find in several of the songs on her debut, it appears that Swift was saying through songs the things that she—the real-life Taylor Swift—had not been able to say verbally when she had the opportunity to do so. Still, Swift's up-front declaration that *Speak Now* focuses on words left unsaid and her advice to her fans to "speak now" suggest a growing maturity.

Ever since the album really started to be taken seriously as an unified art form, especially in the mid- to late 1960s, it seems to have become a foregone expectation of audiences that an album will lead off with one of its best tracks, or at least with something that will stick in the listener's mind and come to define the album. One need only think of the Beatles' *Revolver* and *Sgt. Pepper's Lonely Hearts Club Band*, each of which opened with musicians tuning up and apparently preparing to begin their performance. *Speak Now* has its own kickoff hook. The opening song, "Mine," begins with Swift vocalizing the syllables, "ah, ah, ah," to a simple, brief, distinctive tune and rhythm. Although this does not define the album thematically, it is the kind of unusual effect that immediately captures the listener's attention.

The song contains a couple of memorable lyrical hooks, including Swift's description of herself as "a flight risk with a fear of falling" in the first verse and the chorus line "you made a rebel of a careless man's careful daughter." What is probably most notable about the song, especially given Swift's focus on broken relationships, is that "Mine" highlights reconciliation and the hope of a bright future.

The musical setting of "Mine" contains several notable and appealing features. The first half of each verse section features Swift's low-register, heightened-speech–style phrases. As in her other early songs in which she employs this technique as a writer and singer, this suggests an almost jazz-inspired improvisatory touch. The lower vocal harmony part to Swift's lead in the chorus includes numerous open intervals, which immediately paints the song as part of the country music tradition. Interestingly, Swift makes significant use of the submediant (the minor-quality vi chord) in the song's harmony. This ties "Mine" not only to several other songs on *Speak Now* but also to songs such as "Tim McGraw" (*Taylor Swift*) and "The Best Day" (*Fearless*).

In "Sparks Fly," Swift declares her passion for the intended recipient of the proverbial words left unsaid. In fact, as the album progresses, one can imagine that some of the heartbreak of the later songs might have been the result of the fact that Swift did not express the sentiments of "Mine" or "Sparks Fly" at the time when the relationship(s) was at operating at its peak intensity.

Harmonically, "Sparks Fly" picks up on the hints of the importance of the submediant in the album's opening track. In fact, Swift creates a significant amount of tension between the related major and minor keys of F major and D minor. Although the song seems predominantly to be in the key of F, it ends on the relative minor (D). This ambiguity between the relative major and minor keys not only heightens the importance of the submediant, but it also calls to mind earlier rock styles. Some of the earliest scholarly reviews of the work of Beatles' songwriters John Lennon and Paul McCartney referred to the modal quality of their work, a quality that in part was because of this very type of ambiguity between the prevailing major tonality and its relative minor key. For readers who are interested in trying to hear the connections between "Sparks Fly" and the work of the English quartet that had already been defunct for nearly twenty years before Taylor Swift was even born, the Lennon and McCartney-penned songs on the 1963 album *With the Beatles* is a good place to start.

"Sparks Fly" is a good solid song about passion, with engaging music that could be adapted into a variety of contemporary pop music styles. With minimal references to country music, and with lyrics that by and large fit into conventional phrase structure (in contrast to some of Swift's quirkier and more easily identifiable as "Swiftian" lyrics), "Sparks Fly" seems on many levels to be kind of a song that Swift might have penned as part of the Nashville songwriting establishment, had she not actually become a singing star.

One of the particular features of the song that marks it as a well-thought-out work and that helps to make it effective in this arrangement—and that could easily be included on another version by another performer—is the integration of the vocal melody and the instrumental accompaniment. In particular, on the words "sparks fly," the vocal pitches are used as the starting points for the more elaborate instrumental lick that starts at the beginning of each word. This might not seem like a big deal; however, it is one of the small touches that takes a song such as this one beyond the realm of a set of lyrics set to a particular tune backed by a particular harmonic structure into the realm of a more fully realized conceptual whole—in other words, into the realm of the fully realized composition.

The next track, "Back to December," became one of the album's hit singles. In fact, the song reached No. 6 on the *Billboard* Hot 100, No. 11 on the Mainstream Top 40 chart, and made it into the Top 10 on several airplay charts. On Swift's first two albums, she tended to play the role of the jilted party and the outsider who was kept an outsider by others, be they cheating ex-boyfriends, playground bullies, prettier and more provocative female rivals, and so on. Interestingly, she plays the role—apparently the real-life role—of the jilter in "Back to December," for here she is the one who now regrets having ended the relationship. On the basis of the airplay and single sales success of the song, Swift's new role did not hurt her standing with her audience. In fact, it can be argued that one of the more important aspects of *Speak Now* is that it represented Swift's growing maturity, both personally and as a songwriter. In "Back to December," more so than in the songs of *Taylor Swift* or *Fearless*, she deals with her own past mistakes.

The chorus of "Back to December" has easily the most unusual structure of any of the songs on *Speak Now*. This section is built in two principal subsections, the first of which is eight measures long and the second of which is twelve measures long. However, the total length of these subsections tells only part of the story of the unusual phrase structure of the chorus. The first subsection is divided asymmetrically into a six-measure phrase plus a two-measure tag; the second subsection is built in an asymmetrical 6+4+2 structure. The unpredictable (and slightly unnerving) phrase structure and the syncopation at the level of the sixteenth note within a slow ballad style are reminiscent of some of the works of the songwriting team, Elton John and Bernie Taupin. In fact, listeners who are familiar with Taupin's sometimes quite vivid turns of phrase might detect his possible influence in Swift's text "you gave me roses and I left them there to die."

The song "Speak Now" is framed as a fantasy around what might happen in real life if one were actually to speak up at a wedding when the officiating clergyperson invites members of the assembly to "speak now or forever hold your peace." Swift's playful lyrics represent something of a gender role reversal of the "Elaine!" moment in Charles Webb's 1963 novel *The Graduate*, which was made famous by the 1967 Mike Nichols's film of the same name. In one of Hollywood's most iconic scenes, Dustin Hoffman's character (Ben) repeatedly pounds on the second-floor glass window shouting the name of Katharine Ross's character (Elaine), thereby stopping Elaine's wedding. Ben and Elaine run off together on a passing bus. Taylor Swift's fantasy wedding interruption varies with respect to some details from that of *The Graduate*; however, the two scenes seem to come out of the same basic fantasy theme, reflecting back to the question of what might really happen when someone does indeed "speak now," rather than forever holding his or her peace.

"Speak Now" is also an interesting—and fun—display of Swift's humor. Swift describes the bride's kin as "her snotty little family all dressed in pastel." For the listener familiar with the novel and the two film adaptations, this image suggests a uniformly dressed, neatly suburban collection of *Stepford Wives*-like characters. Even absent any connection that the listener might make between the pastel-clothed family and a dystopian story such as that of Ira Levin's 1972 novel *The Stepford Wives*, the hue of the clothing suggests the neatness and tidiness of suburbia, a world quite different than the world in which Swift's autobiographical characters have tended to fit throughout

Swift's career as a songwriter. Similarly, Swift mocks the bride's gown by describing it as being "shaped like a pastry," thereby getting additional little jabs in.

Given the fact that Swift is credited with the art direction of the CD booklet and given the text of the song, it seems unexpected that the photograph that accompanies the lyrics of "Speak Now" shows the screaming bride dressed in pretty much a conventional wedding dress and the groom and Swift being the characters perhaps most obviously dressed in what could be construed as pastel colors: Swift is pictured in a pink dress (albeit perhaps too vivid to be considered a pastel) and the groom is wearing a light pink shirt. It appears that Swift might have missed an opportunity to extend the joke into the visual realm of the album's booklet.

In his review of the song "Speak Now," *Rolling Stone* magazine critic Jon Dolan noted that Swift quotes the tune to which she set the words "she wears short skirts" in the *Fearless* track "You Belong with Me."[3] Interestingly, elements of this brief melodic motive can be heard in several phrases of the verses of "Speak Now"; however, the quotation, whether intentional or not, might not be entirely obvious unless one compares the two songs side by side. Still, what melodic connection exists in the mind of the listener might contribute to a deeper understanding of subtext in "Speak Now." Specifically, both songs connect clothing and attitude as Swift compares herself to her rivals for the affections of a young man.

Interestingly, the apparent melodic self-quotation in the song "Speak Now" is not the only musical connection between the songs of *Speak Now* and earlier pieces. In fact, *Speak Now* was Swift's most musically referential album up to that point of her career. For example, in several songs one can hear hints the possible influence of the British band, the Police, particularly that band's work from the early 1980s. There are also strong hints of the work and guitar processing of the Edge on U2's album *The Joshua Tree*. In fact, the album's final song seems to exhibit the possible influence of David Bowie's "Heroes." As already mentioned, the major-relative minor ambiguity of "Sparks Fly" might suggest the early music of the Beatles. In the case of "Speak Now," not only do variants on the "short skirts" motive occur in several phrases of the verses, but the chorus also features the drum style associated with the early recordings of the Beatles, both those prefame recordings made when Pete Best was the drummer and the earliest recordings made after Ringo Starr replaced Best (snare drum on beat two, the "and" of two, and on beat four). Significantly, some new wave rock bands of the early 1980s adopted this percussion pattern. The connection to new wave rock is the real significance here, as the aesthetics of the 1980s seem to play such a prominent role in the instrumental tone qualities and musical forms and textures of *Speak Now*. Incidentally, Swift would later fully acknowledge the connections of her work to the music of the decade of her birth with the release of her 2014 album, *1989*.[4]

"Dear John" has been so fully associated with Swift's relationship with singer-songwriter John Mayer that it is difficult to consider the song as anything other than an autobiographical statement about the relationship. One could think of the song as a more generic "Dear John" letter; however, both Swift and Mayer have spoken publicly about the song in such unambiguous terms that the listener might find it difficult to separate the song from Mayer. Certainly, based on the age that gives for herself in the song—19—her relationship with Mayer fits chronologically. The "John" whom Swift addresses in the song seems to be highly egotistical, a trait that Mayer has later acknowledged was a problem for him in the late 2000s, when he had on-again, off-again relationships with Swift, Jessica Simpson, and Katie Perry and made several highly controversial public statements about his sexual prowess.[5] While one might interpret the soft-rock ballad style of the song as suggestive of Mayer's style (at least before he ventured more fully into blues), if the song had different lyrics or was not otherwise connected with Mayer, it seems unlikely that anyone would automatically think "John Mayer" based on the musical setting alone.

For his part, Mayer appeared to have responded to Swift in his 2013 song "Paper Doll."[6] If the listener connects the two songs with the turbulent relationship between Swift and Mayer, one might consider past artist-versus-artist battles in song. Certainly, the breakup of the Beatles was acrimonious, and it generated a brief but nonetheless famous song battle between John Lennon ("How Do You Sleep?") and Paul McCartney ("Too Many People" and "Dear Boy"). Swift's "Dear John" carries with it some of the invective of Lennon's "How Do You Sleep?" especially when she describes Mayer's game-like motives as "dark" and "twisted." What is perhaps most notable—and perhaps most surprising—about "Dear John" is that the song itself represents Taylor Swift's standing up for herself (after the fact) against Mayer, given the time and place. For the time period of *Speak Now* was the time during which it was becoming increasingly common for artist-versus-artist battles to take the form of Twitter wars, or other equally globally followed exchanges through social media. Producing a song that seems so clearly to be about a fellow musician seems to represent Taylor Swift going old school: going back to doing public battle the way that Lennon and McCartney did in the early 1970s on their albums *Imagine* (Lennon) and *Ram* (McCartney).

It should also be noted that "Dear John" is a lengthy song, clocking in at 6 minutes and 46 seconds. Curiously, *Speak Now* contains five songs that are longer than 5 minutes. In fact, this album easily contains the highest concentration of the lengthy songs of any Taylor Swift album to date. Several can be appreciated as big rock anthems on their own; however, having so many long songs means that *Speak Now* does not have as many punchy changes of pace as do Swift's other albums.

As discussed by fans—and entertainment magazine writers—as was "Dear John,"[7] ultimately perhaps the most famous track from *Speak Now* is "Mean."

From a stylistic, production, and musical arrangement standpoint, this overtly country-style song turned out to be something of an outlier on an album that most of the time seems to be more about mainstream rock and mainstream pop than about Taylor Swift's original musical roots. "Mean," though, makes full use of fiddle, banjo, and other instrumental tone colors and textures associated with country music. Further suggesting the country nature of the song is the instrumental slide up a whole-step in open fifths that occurs shortly after the end of each statement of the song's chorus. Although this may be difficult to detect based on technical terms such as "whole-step" and "open fifths," listeners will be guided to exactly where this occurs in the song's official music video, in which the musicians lean toward each other (hint: focus on the fiddle player and Swift) when this musical move takes place, just after Swift sings the question, "why you gotta be so mean?" Incidentally, the whole-step slide up from the lowered-seventh scale-step to tonic implies the use of the Mixolydian mode, a scale that is commonly found in Anglo-American folk music, the root of American commercial country music.

Perhaps to a greater extent than any of Taylor Swift's earlier songs, "Mean" finds her using a short melodic motive to generate much of the catchy chorus. In fact, the fragment to which she set the word "Someday" is essentially the germinating kernel for the entire section. By and large, the other parts of the chorus tune consist of the "Someday" motive reiterated on different pitch levels, inverted, or expanded upon. Like other Swift commercial hits dating back to "Tim McGraw," the chorus of "Mean" has a natural tunefulness and character that seems to invite singing along.

Much of the focus on "Mean," however, has not been on the musical setting; it has been on the lyrics and their theme of empowerment. The song began as a statement against a music critic who criticized Swift's singing technique. Apparently, this pointing out of "flaws" that Swift already recognized affected her deeply, at least if the song's text is taken at face value. She sings of "walk[ing] with [her] head down" and being "wounded." In the chorus of the song, however, Swift shows her resolve by telling her tormenter that someday she will become so big that the critic's words, or presumably those of any critic, will no longer be able to affect her.

Despite the fact that it does not take much digging below the surface to figure out that "Mean" is about a music critic who hurt Swift by writing that "I can't sing," as she states in the song's lyrics, the piece quickly took on a life of its own as an antibullying anthem. In fact, "Mean" became much discussed on various LGBTQ blogs, which helped to cement its status as an antibullying song.[8] So, what is it about an artist's response to an individual critic that allows "Mean" to function effectively as an antibullying song of empowerment for other groups of people? Certainly, Swift's statement that "someday, I'll be big enough that you can't hit me" connotes a sense of empowerment; however, the mass appeal of the song as a stance of empowerment against bullying seems more to be because of the music video—which focuses on this theme—than the song itself. In the video, various young outsiders are seen receiving the derision of their classmates. By the end of the video, each of the outsiders is shown as having achieved their dreams. Although one would have to rely on stereotypes to infer the connection, the appearance of one young male character who is sitting in the school locker room reading a fashion magazine while being tormented by football players (at the song's conclusion, the character is seen presenting a runway fashion show featuring his designs of women's clothing) can be understood as possibly implying an LGBTQ connection with the scenes of junior high and high school bullying that run through the first part of the song.

Much of the focus of commentary on "Mean" has centered on the song's (and the video's) antibullying and empowerment themes. It should be noted, however, that Swift also touches on more familiar country-music themes in the song. In particular, it is significant to note that Swift's character connects success with "living in a big old city." The implication is that moving to the city signifies success, or at least career and financial success. In the context of Swift's increasing move toward pop music, this could be understood as a reference to the pop star moving to Los Angeles or New York—and Swift did move to New York City about four years after the success of this track; however, taken at its least autobiographical point, the implication is that, in more general terms, one must leave the rural country life in order to have truly made it as a success. Significantly, "Mean" is the most overly country-style song on *Speak Now*. This is significant because Swift's connection of success in life with moving to "a big old city" reflects a theme that has been part of Appalachian popular culture for generations. In fact, this notion is the basis of country singer-songwriter Dwight Yoakam's 1987 song "Readin', Rightin', Route 23." As Yoakam tells it in the song—as well as in numerous interviews in which Yoakam has participated—the way out of poverty for Kentucky and West Virginian coal miners and their families was to learn to read and write and, perhaps most importantly, to take U.S. Route 23 north into Ohio. The migration of Appalachians after labor problems, lockouts, strikes, and closures of mines throughout the early 20th century roughly followed this route to Columbus, Ohio, and beyond. As an example of the extent of this migration in the early 20th century, Akron, Ohio, while located considerably east of U.S. 23, was only half-jokingly called the "Capital of West Virginia" because of the number of miners who moved there to work in the tire industry. As a result of this migration, incidentally, Akron became a significant market for country music.

Rolling Stone named "Mean" No. 24 on the magazine's list of the "100 Greatest Country Songs of All Time."[9] This seems to be particularly significant in light of the fact that the ranking was made less than half a decade after the release of the song. Suffice it to say that "Mean" was up against, and was ranked higher than, country recordings with significantly longer track records, thus making Swift's high ranking particularly noteworthy and, perhaps for some readers of the magazine, surprising and at least a little controversial.

As mentioned earlier, some of the songs of *Speak Now* share musical, arrangement, and instrumental tone color connections. As Swift pointed out in her liner notes, they also share a common theme: "things that I could have said but did not say at the time ..." Generally, there are not a lot of clear, direct lyrical connections that suggest that groups of songs are about the same relationship. When these possible connections do occur, it is worth noting, as they tend to stick out as one listens to the tracks. The next song on the album, "The Story of Us," finds Swift addressing a lover in a failing relationship ("the story of us looks a lot like a tragedy now ..."). Although the relationship is clearly on the downhill slide, early in the song, Swift remembers that at one time she thought that the relationship's story would be all about when "we met and the sparks flew instantly," thereby connecting this song to the earlier "Sparks Fly." In fact, one can read the present song as the price that was paid in the relationship because Swift never uttered the sentiments of "Sparks Fly" when she had the chance to do so.

"The Story of Us" was one of the songs that Big Machine Records issued as singles in 2010 and 2011. Although it did make the charts, "The Story of Us" was not nearly as commercially successful as the single releases of "Mean," "Mine," "Speak Now," or "Sparks Fly." Perhaps more than the other songs on the album, "The Story of Us" is not quite as strong in the hook department. The most memorable melodic and lyrical hook is probably the line, "the story of us looks a lot like a tragedy now." This text and the tune to which Swift set it is memorable; however, it is one of the few examples on *Speak Now* of a large amount of text set to rapid rhythm that just does not seem to be as spontaneous or natural sounding as it needs to be in order to be the basis of a true hit song.

The album's next track, "Never Grow Up," truly stands out from the rest of the songs because of its lyrical focus. Here, Swift deals with the concept of growing up, out of childhood, and how it can lead to greater complications in life and a dissolving of some of the intimacy of the parent-child relationship. She begins by playing the role of the mother who asks her baby to "never grow up," presumably so that she (Swift's character) can continue to savor the bond of mother and baby into the future. In the next verse, Swift plays the role of observer. She sees a 14-year-old girl who insists that her mother drop her off around the block from the movie theater, because at that age it is not cool to be seen being dropped off by your parents. At the end of the song, the young girl has grown into a adult woman. As her parents help her move into a new apartment in the big city, the young woman wishes that she had never grown up and out of the innocence and joy of childhood. Although framed around the concept of age, at its core "Never Grow Up" has as its principal themes as the loss of innocence, the ebb and flow of the emotional and spiritual ties between the generations, with a touch of the old saw "be careful what you ask for": independence and social standing within the adolescent community are not necessarily all that it is cracked up to be. To the extent that the song construed as autobiographical, one can only wonder how the sentiments that Swift expresses might pertain to other prodigy artists and especially former child stars.

The simplicity of Swift's melody and the uncomplicated nature of the arrangement and overall musical setting suggest the innocence of the opening scene in the lyrics. It is not quite a lullaby-like tune but could be construed by the listener as a stylized version of a lullaby. The setting captures some of the bittersweet nature of the progression of the story and its themes. "Never Grow Up" is not Taylor Swift's greatest achievement as a songwriter, but it does represent growth, as in this song Swift moves into unfamiliar thematic territory and works within a musical vocabulary that is removed from her usual big-hit hook-driven style. So far, as Swift captures a mood in this song that is outside of the realm of her past work, "Never Grow Up" suggests that her talent as a songwriter might in future successfully venture farther and farther away from the world of obvious autobiography into areas such as film soundtrack work.

In "Enchanted," Swift moves in a direction that is somewhat unfamiliar, particularly based on the bulk of her earlier repertoire, which tended to focus nearly exclusively on broken relationships. Here, she recounts meeting a new love interest for the first time. Swift's use of language in the song (e.g., "it was enchanting to meet you") differs considerably from the more direct language of some of her breakup songs (e.g., "I hate that stupid, old pickup truck you never let me drive"). In fact, the contrast between the images of hurt in the bulk of the song and the romantic, almost old-fashioned use of the word "enchanted" seems to be designed to point out the uniqueness of this chance meeting and how different it is with some of the meetings that have ended in broken relationships.

Although "Enchanted" is not a pop, hook-filled, solid-gold hit like some of Swift's other compositions from around this time period, it is important to note that the song shares some musical traits with some of the other, better-known, and better-remembered songs in the Swift canon. The listener might, for example, detect the move to the minor-quality submediant (vi) chord that seems to run throughout *Speak Now*. This is a song, too, that has an unconventional and unpredictable (at least the first time one experiences it) phrase structure. If anything, the phrase structure is more overtly nonpop song oriented than that of "Back to December." This gives "Enchanted" a feeling of spontaneity and improvisation, even though, in retrospect, the song's structure is actually quite consistent from verse to verse. The spontaneous feel is enhanced by the arrangement of coproducers Nathan Chapman and Taylor Swift, who give the track a deliberately thin, almost demo-track-like sound. Although this contrasts with the rest of the songs on *Speak Now*, it breaks up some of the slickness of the rest of the collection.

In general, the songs on *Speak Now* are clear and unambiguous. "Better than Revenge" stands as something of the exception to the rule; however, only if one perhaps digs too deeply into the ramifications of the lyrics. On the surface, this is a song about one of Swift's female rivals who took a boyfriend away from Swift. The potential challenge for the listener is that Swift sings of her rival that "she's gonna find stealing other people's toys on the playground won't make you many friends." The intent of this observation seems to be to suggest that Swift's rival's actions are akin to those of an elementary school playground bully. The problem is that statement can also be understood as equating the boy for whom the two rivals were vying with a playground toy. This begs the question: Does Swift mean to equate the boy with a childhood toy? Is he just a plaything for Swift and her rival? There is nothing else in the song's text that suggests that Swift/Swift's character might have meant to denigrate the boy in this way, so it appears that the listener should not read this into the song's meaning. However, the turn of phrase does stand out as perhaps the most ambiguous and the most susceptible to misinterpretation on the album.

If the lyrics of "Better than Revenge" sound like they may be among Swift's edgier work on *Speak Now*, the musical setting confirms the edge. This is, in fact, a musical composition and arrangement in the manner of early 1980s rock. In fact, some listeners may hear "Better than Revenge" as a spiritual and musical descendant of Joan Jett's work with the Blackhearts throughout the decade. In fact, the stylistic connections between "Better than Revenge" and Jett's 1990 cover of AC/DC "Dirty Deeds Done Dirt Cheap" are closer than what one might expect, given the high degree of contrast between the musical personas of Jett and Swift. Unlike the AC/DC song—or some of Joan Jett's well-known hard-rock hits for that matter—"Better than Revenge" is built around melodic interest and melodic accessibility as much as it is built around sheer musical and lyrical power. Be that as it may, the musical setting put together by coproducers Swift and Chapman—as well as by the other musicians on the track—is a reasonable example of hard rock. This brings up one of the aspects of Swift's work that was perhaps underappreciated before she began collaborating more extensively with a wider range of artists on *Red* and *1989*: that her studio and live band from the start of her career through *Speak Now* can and did perform with a pretty high degree of authenticity in an unusually wide range of styles.

The next song, "Innocent," can be understood as a statement of support and encouragement. Perhaps the ultimate message is captured by Swift's hidden message (using her standard modus operandi of capitalizing particular letters in the CD booklet's lyrics), "Life is full of little interruptions." The 32-year-old character to whom she sings has apparently made some mistakes and suffers from a degree of self-doubt; however, in the eyes of Swift's character, their "string of lights are still bright ..." Because Swift compares the present reality, the other character's experience, with such images as their "lunchbox days" and their "firefly catching days," the song contains the kind of comparison of adulthood with the innocence and simplicity of childhood that can be heard in "Never Grow Up." On a more global scale, this reflection on the beauty of the past runs through some of the other songs, although in a work such as "Back to December," it is Swift's character that longs to return to the innocence of the past.

The musical setting of "Innocent" is that of a gentle ballad. The song can be construed as a "country" song; however, it is just as much a pop ballad. One of the features that helps the song stand apart from generic ballads is Swift's use of a high degree of rhythmic syncopation in her delivery (one of the standard features of her slow ballads throughout her career). Notable too is the offhanded way in which she sings the lines that contain some of the more vivid images. Listen, in particular, to her casualness as she delivers the references to "lunchbox days" and "firefly catching days." This performance approach lends the song a feeling of authenticity and spontaneity, regardless of how calculated it might be.

Given the fact that *Speak Now* is a wide-ranging album with respect to musical style and tempo, it is difficult to identify particular tracks as outliers. However, with its combination of arena rock and contemporary, big-production, musical theater–style of "Haunted" makes the song stand out from the other songs. Suffice it to say that, at least up to this point of Taylor Swift's career, the primary commercial hooks in her songs tended to revolve around unusual turns of the phrase in her lyrics and catchy, memorable melodic phrases in the lead vocal part. In "Haunted," one of the most easily memorable features is the alternating eighth-note line in the orchestral strings, which combines with the lead electric guitar to form a composite instrumental riff. In addition to being memorable, the riff is dramatic and powerful, in part not only because of Swift's focus on minor harmonies but also because of the arrangement and production. Although the orchestral arrangement by Paul Buckmaster is not as technically challenging as the well-known synthesizer riff that in part defines Billy Joel's 1982 song "Pressure," the dramatic impact of Buckmaster arrangement rivals that of Joel's piece.

In the lyrics of "Haunted," Swift recalls seeing her lover leaving her after "something's gone terribly wrong." Clearly, her character is haunted by seeing the final outcome of the breakdown of the relationship, although Swift seems to studiously avoid actually using the word "haunted" in the lyrics. It takes until the end of the chorus for the word to actually appear for the first time. Compare this to the preceding song, "Innocent," in which Swift sang a fair number of times "you're still an innocent." The avoidance of the title word in the verses and throughout the bulk of the chorus—while simultaneously creating a specter of actually being haunted by the realization that the relationship is ending—suggests a higher level of sophistication than in some of Swift's songs that seem to hammer the title line (or the single word of the title) home. "Haunted" asks more of the listener: to make the connection herself or himself and to actively work to find evidence of the haunting in the song's text.

Another song of lost love, "Last Kiss," finds Swift creating a mood using still different techniques. This song features a minimalistic—and frankly, repetitive—verse melody, but perhaps the most notable feature is the arrangement's use of space to create a sense of passing time without resolution of Swift's sense of loss. What happens is that the instrumental introduction—which dwells on harmony, rather than on a melodic riff—and the similar instrumental breaks in between the vocal parts of the piece are significantly longer and more atmospheric (almost in the manner of late 20th-century trance music) than what is found in more conventional pop songs. In part, this use of musical space is responsible for this ballad lasting for just over 6 minutes.

To any Taylor Swift fan, the theme of "Last Kiss"—that her character continues to remember the couple's last kiss and hopes that her former lover thinks of her—is familiar. The theme, in fact, is at the root of numerous Swift compositions, going all the way back to her first single release, "Tim McGraw." What this song demonstrates is that nearly a half-decade after the aforementioned "Tim McGraw," Swift was still finding new ways to spin the theme.

The album's final track, "Long Live," continues the feeling of a musical homage to 1980s rock, with hints of U2 running throughout the song. Interestingly, the lyrical theme of a couple overcoming odds to receive "[their] trophies" to the outrage of "the cynics" as well as the near anthem-like structure of "Long Live" resembles David Bowie's classic song "Heroes." In fact, if the listener is familiar with the Bowie work, Swift's reference to crashing through walls makes for a particularly strong connection, as "Heroes" revolves around a scene along the Cold War-era Berlin Wall. Swift includes perhaps her most enigmatic "hidden message" capitalized letters in the text: "FOR YOU," suggesting that the recipient will know exactly who he is. Significantly, this expression of appreciation and achievement represents another demonstration of Swift's growth in that it combines the personal and the professional in a way that had not been seen in her previous work. It is, in short, clearly an artist's view of her relationship with another artist. It is important to note this aspect of the song, as it really does represent Swift stepping away from producing autobiographical songs that focused solely on a sense of loss and coming to grips with it, from the perspective of a character that could be virtually any young woman in just about any career. "Long Live" sounds more obviously autobiographical in that Swift's character clearly shares not only the emotions but also the career of the real-life writer of the song.

As has been the case with all of Swift's albums to date, Big Machine Records seemed intent to bring as much added value to CD releases of *Speak Now* as possible. The CD booklet features numerous staged photographs that either recall the official videos for the songs or depict a notable scene from the song's storyline. The color palette used throughout the booklet is rich and varied. In short, it is a visually stimulating package that goes well beyond just presenting song lyrics and songwriting and production credits. Swift herself is credited with the art direction of the booklet. But the booklet is only part of the value-added nature of the enhanced-content version of the album. In addition to the bonus songs "Ours," "Superman," and "If This Was a Movie," the extra bonus disc includes music videos for "Mine," a "pop" mix of "Mine," acoustic versions of "Back to December" and "Haunted," as well as a "on the set," behind-the-scenes documentary film on the making of the "Mine" video.

Let us take a brief look at the three bonus songs that are not otherwise represented on the original, nonexpanded version of *Speak Now*. If the song "Ours" had actually been on the original album, it seems likely that listeners would have detected a relationship with the theme of "Long Live." Both songs have at their core the theme of overcoming the odds and overcoming the objections of others. Musically, however, the two songs stand in sharp contrast, with "Ours" being a gentle mid-tempo ballad. The song sounds as though it could have been an experiment for Swift, as the rhyme scheme is different than those of the bulk of her songs. In "Ours," Swift includes a significantly higher number of hard rhymes at the ends of lines, particularly in the first verse. That verse basically has five lines (depending on how one perceives them), the first, second, third, and fifth of which end with rhymes ("air," "stairs," "stares," and "theirs"). The chorus, the bridge, and other verses do not include as many hard rhymes. The contrast in the use of rhymes from section to section gives the text a feeling of spontaneity, almost in the manner of what one might experience at a poetry slam; however, some listeners might find the opening verse to be a little awkward because of the unusually large number of rhymes in fairly quick succession.

"Superman" represents a very different kind of rhetorical perspective for Swift. Here, she describes a "tall, dark, and super man," whom she longs to "be with . . . someday." Her "Superman" seems to be something of a conventional businessman (e.g., every day "he puts papers in his briefcase and drives away"), not entirely the type of man that has been the object of Swift's desire—or scorn—in her previous songs. Listeners who are familiar with music from the 1980s might be reminded of the male character in Florrie Palmer's composition "Morning Train (Nine to Five)," a hit in the early 1980s for British singer Sheena Easton. Musically, "Superman" is marked by a 1980s new wave rock rhythmic (note the pulsating eighth notes in the accompaniment) and production style. In fact, some listeners familiar with that particular style might hear "Superman" as a cousin of the Prince composition "Manic Monday," which was popularized by the Bangles. In fact, comparison of the two songs is particularly interesting from a rhetorical standpoint: in the Prince composition, the female singer's character expresses her dread of having to go to work on Monday morning, after a night of "getting down" with her lover. The character mentions that she has to work for the two of them. In sharp contrast, in Swift's song, her character watches "Superman" go off to work every day, presumably leaving her at home waiting. Yes, it is quite a different rhetorical scheme than that found in the related Prince composition, and Swift's character in "Superman" stands in sharp contrast to the more generally empowered first-person characters of the bulk of her output, but the Prince and Swift songs make for an interesting pairing. The melody of "Superman" tends to meander more than the tunes of Swift's most commercially and critically successful songs. This, and the unusual rhetorical scheme, make "Superman" sound very much like a song for which its writer had a different singer in mind.

"If This Was a Movie" seems like another example of the kind of song that Swift might have written either for another artist or to be shopped around to other possible performers. Unlike her clearest autobiographical-sounding songs, this is constructed around a more conventional concept and uses a more conventional way of expressing emotions than more distinctive songs on *Speak Now*. The gist of the text is that Swift's character fantasizes that, if real life "was a movie," then her now-gone lover would have apologized for his transgression, Swift's character would have forgiven him, and the two would be back together. It is the metaphor of the movie that seems to be more conventional than some of the quirkier, more Swiftian lyrics of most of the other songs on the album. Personally, I find myself asking why certain tracks are relegated to "bonus" status—not just in the case of Taylor Swift's work, but in the case of all pop musicians whose record companies issue such tracks. "If This Was a Movie" contains an unusual mixture of instrumental tone colors, including distorted electric guitar, a full orchestration, and some of the acoustic stringed instruments of country and folk music. At issue is the fact that the tone colors seem to send the listener mixed-genre messages in this arrangement, something that generally is not the case with the "real" *Speak Now* tracks. The other possible reason that "If This Was a Movie" seems not to have made the cut for inclusion on the original, non-bonus-track release of *Speak Now* might be that in its melodic structure, the song bears some resemblance to the more lyrically distinctive album cut "Innocent." Both songs are built around Swift's fairly standard procedure of contrasting a low-register verse melody built around short motivic figures with a higher-register, more tuneful, and more memorable chorus. In the case of these two songs, the tune in the chorus, albeit not exactly the same, might cause the listener of "If This Was a Movie" to wonder, "hmm, haven't I heard something like this before?"

Speak Now appeared at a curious point in Taylor Swift's career. At around age 16, "Tim McGraw" and Swift's self-titled debut marked her as something of a singer-songwriter prodigy. At around age 18, *Fearless* marked Swift as a bona fide star. *Speak Now* represented maturation in Swift's work, especially since the situations of which she wrote and sang generally matched her age (approximately 20 years old at the time). The references to high school (and even elementary school) are more bittersweet, and some of the songs are almost nostalgic in their reflection back to the simplicity and the innocence of childhood. Unlike its predecessor, the album itself was not a Grammy winner, although Swift won Grammys for Best Country Song and Best Country Solo Performance for the song "Mean." "Mean" also made a strong impact as an anthem of empowerment within the LGBTQ community and even within just a short time after its release was recognized by the editors of *Rolling Stone* as No. 24 on the magazine's list of the greatest country songs of all time.[10] Stylistically, though, "Mean" is a bit of an outlier on *Speak Now*, as the album exhibits numerous connections to rock styles from the late 1970s through the 1980s.

Without question, *Speak Now* was a commercial success. It topped *Billboard* magazine's country albums chart and the *Billboard* 200 (the magazines pop album chart), returning to the No. 1 position on the *Billboard* 200 multiple times over the next several years.[11] In addition, "Speak Now," "Mine," "Mean," "Back to December," and the bonus track "Ours" were all successful hit singles.

As seems to be the norm for many pop artists, the release of *Speak Now* was followed by a lengthy world tour in support of the album. The *Speak Now* tour was quite an elaborate production, owing perhaps more to the musical-theater tradition than to the straight-ahead concert tradition. As All Music Guide critic James Christopher Monger notes in his review of the *World Tour Live: Speak Now* CD/DVD combination package, the performances "closely resembled a high-profile Broadway musical."[12] With all of the elaborate sets, numerous costume changes, dancers, and so on, the tour certainly was spectacular, and the DVD release includes behind-the-scenes documentary footage that illustrates how the performances came together.

Interestingly, in 2011, Big Machine Records released *Taylor Swift: Journey to Fearless*, a concert DVD that was filmed during Swift's first concert tour as a headliner. In contrast to the *Speak Now* tour video, *Journey to Fearless* is a traditional concert video, absent the multitude of costume changes, props, sets, and Broadway-like grandeur. The two videos are so different in style and production from one another—although both share high quality visuals, vocal and instrumental performance, and audio quality—that they complement each other well. For fans who are more interested in Swift's music and perhaps a more personable performance, however, *Journey to Fearless* seems more intimate.

Another 2010 project for Swift was the song "Today Was a Fairytale," which was included in the soundtrack of the film *Valentine's Day*. In addition to providing this song for the movie, Swift acted in *Valentine's Day*. Although I will discuss her acting in Chapter 5, "Beyond Music," let us consider "Today Was a Fairytale" here. Perhaps the first thing that Taylor Swift fans might notice about this song is that Swift portrays a character for whom time spent with her lover "was a fairytale." Given the thematic content of the bulk of Taylor Swift's output up to this point, such a magical positive experience might seem highly unlikely. The jaded listener might even find herself or himself asking, "alright, when is the relationship going to sour and the young man finds his name encrypted into the lyrics of a song as printed in a CD booklet?" It is important to keep in mind that the situation could well be the prelude to a typical Swiftian tale of betrayal and an ultimately failed relationship; however, this is a made-to-order song intended for and used in a particular context in a Hollywood motion picture. Within the context of *Valentine's Day*, the song makes as much rhetorical sense as "Teardrops on My Guitar" makes as an expression of Swift's real-life experiences.

Musically, "Today Was a Fairytale" resembles several songs from the early part of Swift's career. The melody of the verses involves a significant amount of quick syncopation to which Swift set a fair amount of text. The verse melodic material is all in the lower register of Swift's vocal range. This stands in contrast to the longer, slower lines in the higher register that make up the chorus. Interestingly, Swift ties the sections of the song together by setting the title line similarly, whether it appears in the verse or the chorus.

RED

Swift's 2012 release *Red* was called by one critic, specifically *Rolling Stone*'s Jon Dolan, "Joni Mitchell-influenced maturity binge."[13] In the world of singer-songwriters of the 1960s through the present, any comparison or acknowledgment of Joni Mitchell can be taken as high praise. Curiously, on the surface, *Red* seems thematically to fall right in line with Swift's previous albums, especially when one considers Swift's statement in the CD booklet's introductory notes. According to Swift, the songs in the collection represent the red-hot side of love in terms of the emotional intensity of the relationships. As one might expect, the intensity of the relationships chronicled in the songs is matched by the intensity of the feelings of hurt, lost love, abandonment, and so on when the relationships end. As Swift wrote, "My experiences in love have taught me difficult lessons, especially my experiences with crazy love. The red relationships. The one that went from zero to a hundred miles per hour and then hit a wall and exploded. And it was awful."[14] So, although *Red* appears to be framed as a concept album, the concept of intense attraction being followed by an intense sense of loss sounds very similar to the theme that had run through the majority of Taylor Swift's work dating back to the beginning of her career.

Red opens with Swift's composition "State of Grace," a track coproduced by Nathan Chapman and Swift. This is notable as one of the attributes of *Red* is that much of the album is defined by Swift's collaborations with songwriters and producers. Among Swift's collaborators were Dan Wilson, Max Martin, Shellback (real name Karl Johan Schuster), Gary Lightbody, and Ed Sheeran. Still, executive producer and the head of Big Machine Records, Scott Borchetta, was present, as was Nathan Chapman and some of the musicians who had worked with Swift before. The presence of Swedish pop songwriter-producers Martin and Shellback, however, clearly continued Taylor Swift's move from a focus on mainstream contemporary country music toward mainstream pop.

The album's opener continues the homage-to-the-1980s feel of a fair number of the tracks on *Speak Now*. On "State of Grace," the references to 1980s rock include Nathan Chapman's guitar processing, which sounds as though it had to have been inspired by U2's The Edge, as well a melodic and rhythmic feel in the verses that sound reminiscent of some of the hit songs of the Australian band Men At Work (perhaps most notably "Who Can It Be Now?"). Interestingly, Swift sets her text "all we know is touch and go" to a melodic figure that closely mirrors that which songwriters Ben Glover and Josh Wilson used to set the title line in their 2011 Christian rock song "I Refuse," from Wilson's album *See You*.

Despite the similarities between "State of Grace" and rock music of the three decades preceding the song, the album's opening track works well as a prelude that puts the rest of the songs into context. Its contextual role perhaps is best summed up by the last bit of Swift's lyrics, "Love is a ruthless game, unless you play it good and right." The rest of *Red* tends to expound on the ruthlessness of red-hot relationships gone bad.

Speaking of red-hot relationships gone bad, Swift moves directly into that area of thematic focus in the song "Red." Here, among other things, she describes one particularly intense—but ultimately failed—relationship as ". . . driving a new Maserati down a dead end street." If "State of Grace" suggested that the songs of *Red* were going to be similar in texture and style to those of Swift's previous albums, that suggestion is confirmed by "Red," which features an accompaniment texture driven by acoustic stringed instruments, including acoustic guitar, banjitar (or ganjo, as it is given in the liner notes),[15] fiddle, cello, and bouzouki. The country/earlier-Swift-compositions connections are also suggested by the melodic contrast between the verses and the chorus as well as the vocal register that Swift emphasizes in the chorus.

Dan Wilson's production on his collaborative composition with Swift, "Treacherous," provides a subtle transition away from the first two Nathan Chapman-produced tracks. Although the sonic textures of "Treacherous" are not radically different from what might be described as the Taylor Swift sound, there is a space to the production (reverberation) and a different-enough instrumental arrangement and playing style that there is no clear precedent for the song's style on *Taylor Swift*, *Fearless*, or *Speak Now*. Some of Taylor Swift's most commercially successful releases have been songs that practically knock the listener over with instantly identifiable tunes that practically beg the listener to sing along. The list of successful singles from *Red* is lengthy, but does not include "Treacherous." This song, enhanced by Dan Wilson's atmospheric setting of Swift's voice (admittedly, this is not suggestive of, say, Enya's album *Watermark*, but compared with the more direct nature of the bulk of Nathan Chapman's production of earlier Swift tracks, "atmospheric" is one word that comes to mind), although different in character than Swift's earlier successful tracks, works well. In fact, to the extent that the listener responds to the subtlety of the setting and the somewhat muted approach of producer Wilson and performer Swift, "Treacherous" can be heard as an example of an increased maturity in Swift's work as a songwriter and performer.

Swift collaborated with the noted Swedish pop producers and songwriters Shellback and Max Martin in the writing of the next song, "I Knew You Were Trouble." Shellback and Martin also produced the track. Given the commercial success that Shellback and Martin had achieved—both independently and as a production team—with artists such as Pink, Britney Spears, Usher, Maroon 5, NSYNC, and others, one might reasonably expect the team to achieve success with Swift, who was already one of the best-known and most commercially successful musicians of the time. Indeed, "I Knew You Were Trouble" and the other collaborations between Swift and the Swedish duo that were issued as singles made it to or near to the top of the pop charts.

It seems logical that anyone familiar with Taylor Swift's work before *Red*, or even with the *Red* tracks that precede "I Knew You Were Trouble," would be surprised or even shocked the first time they heard the track. It is not only a song with significant and dramatic changes of texture from section to section but also a song that features a hip-hop-influenced percussion part. Listen especially for the syncopated bass drum part, which seems to be designed to rattle the license plate on an automobile with a subwoofer in its trunk as any hip-hop dance track. The changes in texture from section to section are something of a curiosity, as the changes seem not to correspond at all to the cohesive message of the lyrics, a message that is summed up by the song's title. *Rolling Stone*'s Patrick Doyle discussed Swift's new direction in his profile of *Red*. Included in Doyle's article is Swift's revelation that she loves R&B and hip-hop.[16] Clearly, that love of hip-hop manifests itself throughout *Red* and to a significantly greater extent than in any previous Taylor Swift album.

With a variety of producers who tend to work in quite different styles, one might reasonably expect contrast from track to track on *Red*, even given the fact that Swift frames the entire album around a single thematic concept. In fact, what happens is that *Red* is sequenced in such a way that some of the stylistic transitions seem pretty fluid, while others are bigger, more dramatic, and sudden. If the move to "I Knew You Were Trouble" was sudden and unexpected, then the same can be said for the change back to a gentle style for Swift and Liz Rose's song "All Too Well."

"All Too Well" hearkens back to Swift and Rose's early hit "Teardrops on My Guitar." In fact, the melodic range and shape on the text "wind in my hair, and I was there" is reminiscent of the melodic material in "Teardrops on My Guitar" to which Swift and Rose set the text "... I keep singing; don't know why I do." Even more than Swift's earliest songs, though, "All Too Well" is dense with text. In fact, the song seems to approach a spontaneous outpouring of Swift's recollections of a past lover and their times together. The feeling of spontaneity is enhanced by the musical structure of the verse sections of the song. The first verse is eight measures long and is followed by a brief instrumental break. Subsequent verses are an unusual fourteen measures in length, with phrases of four, four, four, and two measures. The fact that the verses are not all the same length and the asymmetry of the longer verses combine to give "All Too Well" nearly a through-composed feel, or at least as through-composed as 21st-century pop songs ever are. "All Too Well" is typical of the songs on *Red* in that it relies heavily on multitrack recording. In fact, the only instrumentalist is Nathan Chapman—who plays acoustic guitar, electric guitar, bass, and drums as well as provides the backing vocals. Some of the album's other tracks include more than just one accompanying musician (and Swift plays acoustic guitar on some songs); however, this is an album that features more overdubs than previous Taylor Swift albums.

A collaborative effort of Swift, Shellback, and Max Martin, "22" represents the aftermath of the numerous breakups about which Swift usually writes. In this song, she and some of the women of her age who have experienced the same sorts of the losses in love dress up and go out partying, looking to "fall in love with strangers." The song contains some of Swift's customary them-versus-us references. Specifically, she decides that the club where she is has "too many cool kids," so she decides that it is best "to ditch the scene." The party-like atmosphere, just the very act of going out clubbing as a way to forget—at least for a while—past heartaches is new for Swift; most of her previous songs found her alone, dreaming of the lost lover, and pondering just what went wrong. Anyway, Swift's character ends up dancing with a young man who "looks like bad news," but whom she (to paraphrase), "has just gotta have." The escapism of the scene that cowriters Swift, Martin, and Shellback create—not to mention the fact that Swift's character in this song seems not to have learned anything from Swift's warnings in songs going all the way back to when she was 15 and 16—ironically makes the Taylor Swift of "22" sound less mature and grounded than the Taylor Swift of learning-to-drive age.

The musical setting of "22" contrasts a singer-songwriter–style acoustic guitar-based arrangement in the verses, with a thicker dance-oriented arrangement in the chorus. The setting actually works quite well in helping to define the lyrics. As much as the hip-hop and alternative rock–influenced syncopated bass drum kicks seem to contradict whatever stereotypes the listener might have about a Taylor Swift sound based on her earlier album tracks, this aspect of the arrangement helps to confirm the club scene in which Swift's character finds herself dancing with an intriguing stranger. Also unusual about "22" is the vocal processing that Martin and Shellback give to Swift's voice. The electronic sound suggests the club music that Swift's character is probably dancing to. Ultimately, the song's situation, the specifics of the lyrics, and the musical arrangement and production create a coherent atmosphere. Perhaps because Swift's character in the song is so different from Swift's past characters, or perhaps because the arrangement and production were so different than what was customary for Swift, the single release of "22" did not seem to resonate with the public particularly well, making it only to No. 44 on the *Billboard* Hot 100.

Swift's longtime producer Nathan Chapman returns to the controls for Swift's composition "I Almost Do." This is a far more conventional song with regard to how it fits into the Taylor Swift canon. Here, Swift's character cannot get her former lover out of her mind, and she suspects that he feels the same way. This provides a thematic connection between "I Almost Do" and Swift's earliest hit, "Tim McGraw." In the present song, however, Swift ponders what she might do if her former lover would ask her if she would like to try again. As the song's title implies, she almost would like to do so. As is so often the case in Swift's songs, her character is caught between what she wants and what she knows that she cannot risk trying again. The seesaw of emotions seems to be clearer in "I Almost Do" than in some of Swift's earlier songs. Interestingly, this tug of war connects this song back to some of the earliest hits in the commercial country music–recording industry. For example, more than just a couple of country recording pioneer Jimmie Rodgers's (1897–1933) compositions found his character battling between the competing forces of the urge to roam (and everything that might imply) and the desire to be at home with family.

The musical setting of "I Almost Do" is also descended from Taylor Swift's classic earlier work. The verses are built from short melodic motives that generally are developed fairly low in Swift's vocal range. The chorus features longer-range—and generally higher-register—phrases. Swift's country/folk roots can be heard in the acoustic guitar parts, which Nathan Chapman provides. Chapman includes suspensions and open string–added notes that can be heard not only in country music but also in the acoustic, introspective singer-songwriter music of the early 1970s. In fact, it can be argued that songs such as "I Almost Do" can be interpreted as part of that introspective singer-songwriter movement that goes back to the work of artists such as James Taylor.

A collaborative effort of songwriters Swift, Max Martin, and Shellback, "We Are Never Ever Getting Back Together" was one of the genuine hits of the album. The single release of the song reached the top of the Hot Country Songs chart, near the top of the Mainstream Top 40, and even touched the Top 10 of the Adult Contemporary chart. Curiously, in Japan, the song continued to make chart appearances into 2015.[17] In this song, producers Martin and Shellback electronically process Swift's voice as they had done in their earlier productions on *Red*. Although this gives Swift a slightly robotic sound—and there has been a considerable amount of discussion, both pro and con, of the robotic sound that electronic processing such as Auto-Tune produces ever since that particular software package became prominent in the late 1990s—here it is not as intrusive as might be. In part, this is because the processing is balanced out by Swift's unprocessed singing of the last line of the chorus as well as her unprocessed speaking of the words "like ever" at the end of the chorus. The spoken snippet plays an interesting role in the song, giving Swift's character not only a bit of a feeling of immaturity but also humanity at the same time.

"We Are Never Ever Getting Back Together" is also an interesting song in how it integrates acoustic guitar-based singer-songwriter textures with the modern hip-hop-influenced thumping bass drum. Based, though, on the structure of the song, the melodic material of the verses and chorus, the harmonic material, and the guitar style, one can imagine "We Are Never Ever Getting Back Together" as a more conventional country textured song, suggesting that other performers—or even Swift herself—could successfully incorporate the song into their repertory in a less overtly modern-sounding style and texture. However, the flexibility of Taylor Swift's songs really is nothing new: many of her hits can be interpreted with rock instruments and rhythm section work or country instruments and rhythmic approaches and work equally as well. Interestingly, the adaptability of Swift's compositions seemed to have been increasingly noted by her fellow performers. As will be detailed in Chapter 6, "The Singer or the Song?" by the time of Swift's 2014 album *1989*, a variety of artists were creating effective arrangements and adaptations of Swift's songs that sometimes stood in sharp stylistic and genre contrast to Swift's originals.

As I pointed out earlier, one of the notable features of *Red* is how it sometimes eases the listener from one style to another and sometimes jerks the listener from one style to another. The electronic vocal processing and thumping bass drum of "We Are Never Ever Getting Back Together" is followed by Nathan Chapman's production of Swift's "Stay Stay Stay." In contrast to its predecessor, and several other *Red* tracks, "Stay Stay Stay" barely made it onto the record charts. This is unfortunate, because it is an engaging song that combines Swift's country side with her apparent fascination with pop music of the 1980s. In fact, this fast-tempo song suggests elements of the music of Dolly Parton, 1980s groups such as Culture Club, and the memorable imagery and turn of the phrase that helped Taylor Swift to become a near-instant star singer-songwriter.

Gary Lightbody (of the U.K. band Snow Patrol), Swift, and Jacknife Lee (frequent producer of Snow Patrol's recordings) collaborated in writing "The Last Time." Although the orchestration and the placement of the orchestral instruments in the recording's mix are more muted than what one generally finds in the music of the 1970s, early-1980s group Electric Light Orchestra, the spirit of ELO, as it was also known, might be detected by some listeners in the song's texture and in its harmonies. In particular, ELO songwriter-singer-producer Jeff Lynne tended to favor motion from the tonic (I) chord to the submediant (vi) chord in ELO's songs. This harmonic motion also occurs at the beginning of the so-called oldies progression, the I–vi–IV–V pattern whose popularity among popular songwriters dates back to the 1938 song "Heart and Soul," with music by Hoagy Carmichael and lyrics by Frank Loesser. The reader might recall that several of Taylor Swift's early songs were built around the progression, including "Tim McGraw" and "The Best Day." So, it is not the I–vi motion in and of itself that might conjure up the music of ELO; it is the harmonic motion within the context of the use of orchestral stringed instruments that may cause some listeners to make the connection.

Interestingly, "The Last Time" is a breakup song that features both Swift and Gary Lightbody singing lead vocals. Lightbody's character first presents his view of the failing relationship; then Swift's character presents her view in the second verse. Evaluating the appropriateness of the combination of vocal style, melodic content, and meaning is subjective. However, for this writer, Lightbody's approach seems to fit the song better than Swift's approach. What Swift does bring to what is otherwise very much a ballad is a sense of urgency in her singing. Some listeners might find that a sense of resignation might fit the lyrics better.

The next track, "Holy Ground," is a solo Swift composition; however, unlike the bulk of the solo compositions on *Red*, multi-instrumentalist and Kanye West's sometimes collaborator Jeff Bhasker produced this song. Despite Bhasker's association with West and the world of hip-hop music, "Holy Ground" receives a straight-ahead country-rock treatment. Because the single release of the song did not rise particularly high on the charts, it might be easy to overlook this track. That is especially a concern given that listeners today tend to be more track oriented than the album-oriented listeners of the predownload days and because overlooking "Holy Ground" would be a loss for Taylor Swift fans. In part, because of Jeff Bhasker's production and instrumental work, and the track's arrangement, "Holy Ground" represents a take on the country-pop tradition that had not really been found before in Swift's recordings.

Swift's lyrics in "Holy Ground" also represent something of a new approach for the songwriter. In this song, Swift reminisces about a past lover and relationship, recalling specific events, some of which might seem trivial to anyone other than Swift's character and her counterpart. She then characterizes the ground on which they stood as "holy ground," thereby giving the relationship a sense of the spiritual. Swift tells her ex-lover that "tonight I'm gonna dance . . . but I don't want to dance, if I'm not dancing with you." The lyrics convey a bittersweet mood in Swift's character. What is absent—that sometimes would be found in her breakup songs—is any imparting of blame. Instead, there is almost a sense of melancholy in the wake of the breakup.

The musical setting of "Holy Ground" is pleasant and does represent a twist on country pop; however, the upbeat nature of the music seems to be at odds with the sentimentality and the near-spirituality that Swift expresses in the lyrics. Somehow, and probably because of the engaging pop hooks in the music, it works. That being said, it seems as "Holy Ground" is one Taylor Swift song that would be ripe for other artists to cover as a slower ballad. Swift's recording is not so well known that her version is necessarily as definitive as is the case with her biggest hits, and the melody, harmony, and rhythm of the song could translate well into a ballad tempo.

Another solo composition, "Sad Beautiful Tragic" extends the move in the direction of lyrical impressionism that Swift took on *Red*. Although this is another reaction to a broken relationship, the combination of images and the variety of the ways in which Swift transitions from image to image provides an alternative to her more straightforward pre-*Red* songs. It can be argued that artistic growth is necessary for any artist to remain fresh and relevant as well as to transcend the transitory one-minute-you're-in/next-minute-you're-out world of pop music. The growth as a lyricist—dealing with similar subjects but in a variety of diverse ways—that one can hear on *Red* seems to raise Swift's work to a higher level.

The musical setting of "Sad Beautiful Tragic" features a compound duple meter feel (e.g., two pulses per measure with each divided into thirds, or 6/8 meter). This is notable, as it is not a metrical feel that is frequently found in Swift's songs. Producer/multi-instrumentalist Nathan Chapman, who overdubbed all of the instruments on this track, creates an atmospheric setting that suggests contemporary singer-songwriter folk music, as opposed to the country leanings of many Taylor Swift songs that focus on acoustic instruments. This style, the intimacy of the arrangement and the way in which Chapman set Swift's voice in the recording's mix, the mood of the lyrics, and the somewhat impressionistic style of the lyrical writing all are in synchronism, as opposed to, say, "Holy Ground," in which the tempo seems to be at odds with the bittersweet sentiments of the text.

Some listeners might find that the arrangement and production that Jeff Bhasker provides for Swift's next solo composition, "The Lucky One," not to be so successful. Although the arrangement never really intrudes on Swift's voice, Bhasker's use of a drum machine is unfortunate. Swift's lyrics present a putdown of a woman who, during her school days, was "cool" and "pretty," essentially one of the beautiful people that have been a thorn in Swift's side as a songwriter throughout nearly all of her career. This woman who looks "like a '60s queen" basically made it big in the world, left town, moved to Los Angeles ("the angels' city"), and became too self-important for any of her former friends. Swift's reference to the character as looking "like a '60s queen" practically invites a musical setting that emulates pop-rock music of the 1960s. Jeff Bhasker's drum machine programming calls to mind drum patterns of that decade; however, the mechanical perfection of the programmed pseudo-percussion seems cold in comparison to the rest of the accompaniment.

The young (born 1991) eclectic singer-songwriter Ed Sheeran collaborated with Swift in the writing and performance of "Everything Has Changed." This song also brings another producer, Butch Walker, into the mix. Although Walker includes a touch of modern pop texture in the song in the form of trunk-rattling deep bass drum, this is a mid-tempo ballad that comes closer to the acoustic singer-songwriter style than it does to hip-hop. Swift and Sheeran alternate lead vocals, and their vocal textures and styles match well. Both singers convincingly portray characters who are just beginning their relationship together. The music itself is classic Taylor Swift, with a high degree of syncopation at the sixteenth-note level and a chorus melody that in form and shape calls to mind Swift's work going all the way back to her debut album. Despite the fact that the song is jointly credited to Swift and Sheeran, the verses, too, contain some typically Swiftian attributes, including unexpected lengthening and truncations of phrases. Perhaps because of the primarily acoustic setting, and maybe because of the fact that "Everything Has Changed" is closer to conventional start-of-relationship material than the standard Taylor Swift song, the single release of "Everything Has Changed" was not a huge chart success. It is a pleasant track, though, and should not be overlooked.

On Taylor Swift's pre-*Red* albums, the primary guitarist had always been Nathan Chapman. In fact, even on *Red*, the Chapman-produced tracks also include Chapman as the principal or sole guitarist. Studio musician Dann Huff coproduced the song "Starlight" with Chapman and Swift and performed the song's electric guitar solo. This song represents Swift's character's reminiscences of the time she met her lover in the "summer of '45." The two danced that evening "like [they] were made of starlight." As so often tends to be the case with Taylor Swift's compositions, "Starlight" is a pleasant song, vaguely contemporary country pop in nature. What is a bit unusual is that the verses of the song are more conventionally tuneful than in the songs that Swift wrote earlier in her career, back when the emphasis seemed to be on building verse melodies from short motives, often in a low part of Swift's vocal range. Here, the tunefulness of the verses does not contrast with the character of the chorus as much as might have been the case several years before. Although it can be argued that a less distinctive and more conventional songwriting approach such as that represented by "Starlight" makes Swift's work on *Red* seem somewhat less musically distinctive than her earlier work, it also represents a broadening of songwriting technique. To put it another way, although "Starlight" might be more like mainstream pop music by other artists, the song shows that Swift could write convincing mainstream pop without using just the old Swift modus operandi.

Because *Red* can be interpreted as an exploration of any number of unrelated broken romances and broken relationships, it may be difficult for the listener to detect any sort of overarching narrative flow. Despite the fact that it is more an album of individual songs around the same basic theme than an album built around a linear timeline, the closing track, "Begin Again," does seem like a logical conclusion. In this song, Swift continues the focus of "Everything Has Changed" and "Starlight" on the start of a new relationship free of any of the baggage that tainted earlier failed relationships. So, in the end, the album has a general thematic shape. It begins with an exploration of the intensity of new relationships, moves into explorations of red-hot relationships gone bad, and concludes with an exploration of new relationships that seem to be based more on romance than just sexual attraction and intensity. One could, perhaps, interpret the shape of *Red* as suggesting that Swift's character learned something from the fact that her earlier red-hot relationships ended up crashing and burning with the intensity with which they began; she now focuses on building something deeper and potentially more lasting.

In any case, "Begin Again," a Taylor Swift composition and Dann Huff, Nathan Chapman, and Swift production, takes Swift back to her country roots. The song also features Swift's wide-ranging and free-ranging lyrics as her character explores the ways in which her new potential lover differs from the men with whom she has experienced unsuccessful relationships in the past.

When experiencing *Red* as a single whole entity, one must keep in mind that it is a mammoth album. The sixteen songs that made the cut for the album were all on the original release—this was not like previous Taylor Swift albums that grew to the size of *Red* only when all of the bonus tracks were released in subsequent enhanced editions. Because the album is so lengthy, it is easy to pick and choose tracks to create a playlist of favorites. Because Swift and her producers explore so many different musical styles and textures, though, picking and choosing tracks probably means that something that is worth listening to—and maybe worth deeper consideration—will be left out. The album might not follow a strict narrative curve, but there is evidence of an overall shape. The fact that *Red* explores so much musically but ends with a straightforward country song is also significant, in that "Begin Again" confirms the importance of Taylor Swift's musical roots.

It is also worth noting how *Red* is packaged. The photographs, graphic style, and presentation of the lyrics contrast dramatically with Swift's previous albums. Sure, the "coded" messages are still contained in the capitalized letters in the lyrics (although this seems to be getting stale by the time of *Red*), but the CD booklet is all about a mature young woman with real-life experiences that she plays out in song. Also significant is the fact that the booklet contains no photographs of Swift's accompanying musicians and producers. For one thing, there are probably too many of them, but the other thing that this seems to symbolize is the focus on Swift as a star, with the other heavily overdubbed contributors playing generally purely supporting roles. In some respects, the reliance on contemporary dance rhythms and production styles in some of the songs and the reliance on studio overdubs make *Red* seem at times less immediate and less personal than some of Swift's earlier work.

However, the situations and emotions of her lyrics make many of the songs seem more believable and less calculated than some of her earlier songs.

Perhaps because of the acclaim that Swift's 2014 album *1989* received, it is easy to overlook *Red*. Indeed, in light of the 1980s dance music influence that runs throughout *1989*, *Red* can be viewed in retrospect as a transitional album. To think of "transitional" as a reason to dismiss *Red*, however, would be a mistake, as *Red* contains musical and lyrical moments that stand up to repeated hearings. *Red*, too, represents in several songs a maturing of Swift in terms of her view of relationships and the increasingly subtle way in which she deals with relationships.

In addition to releasing *Red* in 2012, Swift had two songs included in the soundtrack album for the film *The Hunger Games*: "Safe & Sound" and "Eyes Open." Both of the songs were included on the film's soundtrack album, *The Hunger Games: Songs from District 12 and Beyond*; however, "Safe & Sound," a collaborative effort of Swift, the Civil Wars (Joy Williams and John White), and T-Bone Burnett, was only Swift song included in the film itself; "Eyes Open" was one of several songs on the album that was inspired by *The Hunger Games*.

"Safe & Sound" returns Taylor Swift to her country roots; however, the song is more in keeping with the work of her collaborators Williams and White when they were working as the duo known as the Civil Wars than a return to Swift's country-pop-rock style of the late 2000s. In fact, a song such as one written, recorded, and released during a time period in which Swift was moving away from country music in a major way illustrates the extent to which she has been able throughout her career to adopt a range of styles and make them her own. The foray into acoustic folk-country was successful: in 2013, "Safe & Sound" won the Grammy for Best Song Written for Visual Media. "Safe & Sound" is used several times in *The Hunger Games* film. All Music Guide critic Heather Phares describes the song as the one piece on the soundtrack album that is "most crucial to the book."[18] It is important to note that Phares's words come from a review that is highly favorable of many of the other tracks on the album. Despite the importance of "Sights & Sounds" to the narrative of the story, however, the lyrics of reassurance in the face of danger and the gentle musical setting led by John White's guitar and T-Bone Burnett's arrangement and production do not necessarily have to be tied to *The Hunger Games*. The song can function effectively entirely outside the context of the film, providing that one does not associate "Sights & Sounds" with the film because of having seen the movie.

"Eyes Open," a solo Swift composition that finds her working again with long-time producer Nathan Chapman, is a rock song that moves toward the country-rock style of some of Swift's songs of the previous eight years. The instrumental setting might be a little more incisive than earlier arrangements by Chapman, but "Eyes Open" sounds more like the work of the Swift of old than the more dance rhythm-oriented Swift of 2012 or the acoustic folk style of "Sights & Sounds." More than "Sights & Sounds," the lyrics of "Eyes Open" suggest the narrative of the dystopian book and movie *The Hunger Games*. What might be of surprise to listeners the first time they hear the song is that the vocal melody and Swift's singing style do little to suggest the sense of danger and the sense of the dramatic of the lyrics. Arguably, Swift's 2014 collaboration with Ryan Tedder, "I Know Places," is a more tightly matched set of dramatic lyrics and music and more effective at conveying a sense of danger and impending doom within a dystopia. Still, "Eyes Open" was reasonably successful as a single, although certainly not one of Taylor Swift's biggest hits.

1989 and Beyond

4

In this, the most recent phase of Taylor Swift's career, Swift continued her move away from overt connections to country music. In fact, her most recent album to date, *1989*, features a musical and arrangement focus that clearly comes from her collaborations with dance music producers, programmers, and multi-instrumentalists. In addition, Swift's work continued to mature and in a variety of ways. The high school–focused persona that emerged in some of her earlier work—particularly on *Fearless*—was replaced by characters that are closer to Swift's actual age. Although some of Swift's most recent work remains largely autobiographical sounding, some of songs from this phase of her career were more metaphorical and less obviously autobiographical. This has allowed some of her work to fit into a wider variety of contexts, such as in motion-picture soundtracks.

In 2013, Swift collaborated with indie rock singer-songwriter Jack Antonoff on the song "Sweeter than Fiction," a mainstream rock piece that stylistically is more reflective of pre-*Red* Taylor Swift than the music that immediately followed "Sweeter than Fiction" on the album *1989*. The song contains a few Swift signifiers, such as the repeated "I, I, I," which might remind listeners of the "ah, ah, ah" on Swift's earlier song "Mine," or the repeated notes at the opening of the *1989* track "How You Get the Girl." The song is also tuneful in the manner of early Swift hits, and the rock style of the song calls to mind a bunch of the up-tempo songs that Swift recorded back when she worked exclusively with producer Nathan Chapman.

In a brief video documentary about the inspiration for the song, Swift stated, "Getting to see the struggles and triumphs of someone who's never stopped chasing what he was after really inspired me."[1] In fact, Swift went into the project knowing that "Sweeter than Fiction" would be used in the film *One Chance*, the story of British opera singer Paul Potts who won the first *Britain's Got Talent* television competition. Potts had turned to singing as an escape from the pain of being bullied when he was a child and youth. This aspect of Potts's biography must have resonated strongly with Taylor Swift, who had devoted a significant chunk of the album *Fearless*, as well as the song "Mean" and the "Mean" music video, to the subject of bullying.

In the lyrics of "Sweeter than Fiction," Swift addresses Potts, although not by name. She acknowledges the struggle that Potts undertook overcoming bullying and laughter at his attempts to make a go of it as an amateur opera singer. She also addresses the lack of self-confidence that nearly caused Potts to withdraw from trying to take his singing to the next level through competition. In real life, it was the dream of winning the Simon Cowell-produced *Britain's Got Talent* that finally allowed Potts to garner confidence in his abilities, although Swift's song does not drill that deeply into specifics. In fact, had Swift done so, the song might have worked within the context of the film *One Chance* but probably would not have been particularly effective outside the confines of the film. As it turned out, the single release made the charts but—for a Taylor Swift single—was not a huge commercial success. In any case, in the song Swift portrays a character that is not just an outside observer of the Potts story; her character is one of the few people who believed in the character to whom she sings during the time in which he was struggling with self-doubt and lack of success.

1989

In February 2016, Swift's *1989* won the Grammy Award for Album of the Year making Swift the first woman ever to win twice in that category. The album also won Best Pop Vocal Album, and the song "Bad Blood" won the Grammy for Best Music Video. The Grammy success of *1989* makes the album very tricky to assess and to discuss for some critics and fans. The Recording Academy (the organization that awards the Grammys) might have lavished praise on the album by virtue of the organization's Grammy Awards, but critics had differing views of *1989*. For example, *Billboard* magazine's Jem Aswad wrote a generally highly favorable review of the album.[2] On the other hand, All Music Guide critic Stephen Thomas Erlewine complained that the production style and emphasis on contemporary dance club rhythms on the album made Swift the singer and her songs sound somewhat generic on *1989*. In fact, Erlewine's summation of the album was that it was "a cold, somewhat distant celebration of all the transient transparencies of modern pop, undercut by its own desperate desire to be nothing but a sparkling soundtrack to an aspirational lifestyle."[3]

In the foreword to the CD booklet, Swift acknowledges her need to adopt "a new style of music" and that her aim for *1989* was to focus on musical styles from "the decade in which I was born."[4] Swift also acknowledges the importance of her move to New York City in developing the album, its songs, and its style. In fact, Swift had been dropping hints in interviews and on her website in the time leading up to the release of the album that it would be quite different in style from any of her previous albums.

1989 opens with "Welcome to New York," a title that is particularly appropriate given Swift's move to New York City in 2014. Despite any misgivings that Taylor Swift fans might have with her move from country to more mainstream pop, "Welcome to New York" is an engaging, popular, and very interesting song within the Swift canon. This Taylor Swift-Ryan Tedder collaborative piece opens with drum machine and synthesizers that call to mind some of the 1980s work of artists from Prince to Cyndi Lauper. Although Swift characteristically built the verses of some of her early hit songs on brief motives, "Welcome to New York" is almost entirely—verses and chorus—built around repetitions of a single pitch. The bridge section contrasts, and the repeated pitches certainly do not represent all of the melodic material of the verses and chorus, but this is the most monothematic song that Swift has issued to the public through the present. As one might expect, there has to be some other kind of hook to drive the commercial popularity of the piece. The rhythmic material, the synthesizer figures, the electronic processing of Swift's voice, and the sheer catchiness of the repetitions of the title line are all the kinds of hooks that have made this song one of Swift's biggest hits.

Not only does Swift celebrate the bright lights, the hustle and bustle of the city, and the excitement of moving into her new apartment in one of the most iconic cities in the world, she also celebrates the diversity of the people she encounters in New York. In one notable phrase, Swift sings ". . . you can want who you want, boys and boys, and girls and girls." Some fans took this as an acknowledgment of the LGBTQ-friendly nature of New York City, while others understood the text as being supportive of the rights of gays and lesbians (including marital rights), as detailed in a *Time* article by Daniel D'Addario.[5]

"Welcome to New York" received a somewhat mixed reaction from music critics and fans. Writing for Time.com, critic Nolan Feeney compared the song to a "peppermint latte." Although he complained about the arrangement's use of "cheesy synthesizers," he acknowledges that the upbeat nature of the track presents the listener with an optimistic image of New York City from the viewpoint of a "fresh-off-the-bus New York transplant."[6] Time.com's Daniel D'Addario discussed the criticism that the song had received for what some heard as a "lifeless" portrayal of New York. As D'Addario points out, Swift responded to this criticism by donating all of the proceeds from the song to the New York City public schools.[7] When I hear the song, I do not hear it as lifeless, although the 1980s-influenced dance style does not seem as immediate and personal as Swift's country songs. I hear the song as celebratory—albeit with the proverbial rose-colored glasses—and find that the image of the "fresh-off-the-bus New York transplant" that Feeney describes rings true.

Swift reunites with *Red* collaborators Max Martin and Shellback for "Blank Space." This song ticks virtually all of the proverbial boxes with respect to what listeners had come to expect from Swift. The lyrics find her character becoming entranced with a man who is about to become "[her] next mistake," following in the lines of earlier Swift songs in which her character fell in love with the wrong person. This sentiment is confirmed by the chorus's "Boys only want love if it's torture." The melody of the verses is constructed from short motives, another trait that goes all the way back to Swift's debut album. Although the chord progression does not use the entire oldies progression to the extent of, say, "Tim McGraw," the verses open with the tonic (I) chord followed by the submediant (vi) chord, in the manner of "Tim McGraw" and more than just a few Taylor Swift compositions.

The newness of "Blank Space" comes primarily from the work of the track's producers Max Martin and Shellback. Martin and Shellback provide some obvious electronic processing to Swift's voice, which can be understood as a nod to the 1980s influences that run throughout *1989*, or as a nod to the 21st-century fascination with the possibilities offered by music-processing software and hardware such as Auto-Tune. Although the obvious drum machine tones fall in line with the 1980s focus of the album, some listeners might find it less than fully satisfying. And, this represents one of the listener's major challenges with respect to *1989*: some of the producers' use of technology leans in the direction of the mechanical—perceived by some listeners as dehumanized—even though Swift's lyrics sound deeply human, deeply personal. The conflict between the two can be problematic.

In contrast, "Style," a collaboration of writers Swift, Shellback, Max Martin, and Ali Payami, deliberately revolves around style over substance. Swift sings about her lover's "James Dean" looks and her adoption of the "red lipstick thing" that he likes. Because of the lyrical content, the disco/new wave dance arrangement and style works well. The song's melodic and harmonic materials do not necessarily seem to quote any one particular artist of the 1980s; however, all of the musical, arrangement, and production work on "Style" clearly bears the stamp of 1980s influence.

As a song that can be understood as an endorsement, a celebration, of style over substance, "Style" might surprise a lot of Taylor Swift fans. This was, after all, the singer-songwriter who called out the popular girls and the egotistical boys for their superficiality on *Taylor Swift, Fearless, Speak Now*, and *Red*. In "Style," the woman who once compared her blue jeans-wearing character favorably to the girl who "wears short skirts" is now the one who wears the "tight little skirt." The song raises the question: Has Taylor Swift (the person) changed, or has she broadened her writing to allow her to portray a wider range of characters and character types? Some fans may find themselves scouring *1989* for clues as they listen to subsequent tracks, because Swift's character in "Style" stands in such sharp relief to the more autobiographical-sounding characters from her previous work. Listeners seemed not to have been too shocked by the apparently new Taylor Swift persona: "Style" eventually topped the Adult Contemporary and Mainstream Top 40 charts.

Some of the *1989* CD booklet photographs suggest that this is not necessarily meant to be the most serious collection of songs ever assembled. Some aspects of the album, including the references to 1980s dance music that run throughout, seem lighthearted. This does not necessarily move in the direction of parody; however, one probably cannot experience *1989* without at least considering that there may be some deliberate playfulness in everything from the musical arrangements to certain turns of phrase in the lyrics. Even the title of the album—despite the fact that on the surface level it simply represents the year of Taylor Swift's birth—seems as though it might have at least in part been inspired by the title of a 1980s album: Prince's *1999*. Perhaps it is more than just a bit of a stretch—primarily because there is an old expression about being "out of the woods"—but some listeners looking for 1980s references might interpret the title of "Out of the Woods" as a sly reference to the Stephen Sondheim musical *Into the Woods*, a product of the 1980s.

"Out of the Woods," a collaboration of Swift and multi-instrumentalist singer-songwriter Jack Antonoff, is one of the more interesting songs on *1989* with respect to its relationship to previous Swift compositions and in its sonic effects. The long-time Taylor Swift modus operandi of melodic construction—but certainly not characteristic of all of Swift's previous songs—was to build verse melodies from repetitions, sequential statements (starting on different pitch levels), and manipulations of brief motives, or what might be called fragments. "Out of the Woods" has a more conventional verse structure, with each verse consisting of four phrases in an ABAB melodic relationship. To put it another way, it is more conventionally tuneful and a touch more expansive than many earlier Swift verses. In earlier songs, Swift would from time to time use asymmetrical phrase structures or unconventionally rhymed—or unrhymed—pairings of lines. These techniques give some of her songs a feeling of improvised spontaneity, despite the fact that close study of those songs suggests that the apparent spontaneities may actually be completely thought out. "Out of the Woods" follows in this tradition, with a free approach to rhyme in the verses and chorus. In fact, it is probably safe to say that the text in this particular song is about as far away from that of the stereotypical cookie-cutter pop song as one might imagine coming from the pen of a pop star. Interesting, too, about this song is that although it includes some sampling-style effects, the entire package is better integrated than had been the case with some of the songs of *Red* in which the dance rhythms and subwoofer-thumping bass drum sometimes seem more intrusive than integrated.

Although Swift's liner notes for *Red* and for *1989* inform the listener that each collection was conceived as a concept album, musical, lyrical, and structural connections generally are easier to detect on *1989* than on its prede-cessor. One example is the free approach to rhyme in the next track, Swift and Max Martin's "All You Had to Do Was Stay." This immediately calls to mind the lyrical approach of "Out of the Woods." Interestingly, the melodic approach on "All You Had to Do Was Stay" calls to mind the earlier "Wel-come to New York." Specifically, a significant part of the verse melody of "All You Had to Do Was Stay" is built around repeated pitches; however, this is even more pronounced in the chorus.

"All You Had to Do Was Stay" opens with what sounds like 1967-era back-ward tape manipulation. Interestingly, the sounds of the psychedelic 1960s made something of comeback in the 1980s. Perhaps one of the better-known examples from the decade of Taylor Swift's birth of the 1980s fascina-tion with the psychedelia of nearly two decades before was Prince's album *Around the World in a Day.* After the psychedelic-style introduction, the musical setting and arrangement of "All You Had to Do Was Stay" remain tied to the 1980s, particularly in its use of old-school-sounding synthesizers.

The theme of "All You Had to Do Was Stay" is completely captured by the song's title. Despite the fact that the theme of the man in Swift's life leaving was by this point quite familiar in her recorded output, and despite the obvious references to the musical trends of a quarter-century earlier, the song is one of the most immediately engaging since Taylor Swift's big hits from the first several years of her career. With some artists, the problem with a track such as "All You Had to Do Was Stay" is that it would be overlooked. This particularly is true in the case of material by artists whose music primarily is downloaded on a track-by-track basis. Fortunately for this song, although Taylor Swift's singles do sell well and often rise quite highly in the charts, her albums sell very well. What perhaps is most significant, though, is the fact that sales of physical discs are stronger among Swift's fans that typically seems to be the case. Because of this, a fine album cut is less likely to be overlooked in today's download, track-oriented music industry.

While of the subject of album cuts and hit singles, it should be noted that next song on *1989*, Swift, Martin, and Shellback's "Shake It Off," was one of Swift's major hits. The song is constructed in a similar manner to Swift's hits from the beginning of her career: the verse melody is built from repeti-tions and variations of a short motive, and the chorus is in a higher register and more conventionally "tuneful." Interestingly, the arrangement features saxophone as well as more minimally used trumpet and trombone. The horn section, and especially the saxophone part that opens the track, provides a sound not experienced before on a Taylor Swift recording. The repeated tones in the saxophone and the motivically based vocal melody recall the minimal-ism that enjoyed a brief period of popularity in the early 1980s. The reader may want to investigate works such as Laurie Anderson's 1981 song "O Superman (For Massenet)" and Philip Glass's 1982 album *Glassworks*. Ander-son's experimental song made a surprisingly strong showing on the charts, and Glass's album made it onto the jazz, classical, and pop charts, a rare achievement. Although "Shake It Off" clearly does not embrace classical minimalism to the extent of these earlier works, some listeners might perceive a stylistic connection to this early 1980s genre.

The horn section also moves this particular song in the direction of mainstream pop music to a greater extent than other Swift recordings. However, perhaps the greatest reason for the song's pop success is the chorus hook, which is as memorable as anything Swift has recorded to date. The title line, in particular, is one of those melodic fragments that tends to stick with the listener.

The "Shake It Off" video is unusual in that it employed professional dancers, Swift in a somewhat self-effacing guise, as well as some of Swift's real-life fans. An outtake video, which is available via a link from Billboard.com, shows the fans learning for the first time from Swift herself that they were called together to participate in the "Shake It Off" video.[8]

Interestingly, in this "outtake" video, which is really a brief documentary about the making of the official music video for the song, Swift reveals a bit about her lyrical inspiration for the song. She tells the fans who appeared in the video that she had learned, after years of hearing and reading about her music and her performance from critics, that she needs to shake off the criticism—basically, not to take it to heart. This suggests a growing maturity from the Taylor Swift of "Mean" and some of her other pre-*1989* songs in which she expresses very clear frustration and hurt at the words and actions of others. However, the attitude that Swift expresses on "Shake It Off" does not run consistently throughout the album. On "Bad Blood," for example, Swift's character clearly holds onto the hurt that she says that she has learned to let go of in "Shake It Off."

Swift and Jack Antonoff collaborated in writing "I Wish You Would." Perhaps one of the most notable features of this song is the duo's approach to rhyme. The verses and the chorus begin in a similar manner to songs such as "All You Had to Do Was Stay" and "Out of the Woods," in other words, in apparently free verse. When the rhymes occur, they do so at the very close of the verses and the chorus. This unexpected twist tends to suddenly snap the listener to attention.

The Swift, Max Martin, and Shellback collaboration "Bad Blood" turns *1989* in the direction of hip-hop. There is very little about the composition itself, the arrangement, or even the vocal style to suggest to someone who had never heard the song before that it is a Taylor Swift song. Certainly, the theme of two people who have parted company in a less than amicable way having "bad blood" between them had been part of the Swift repertoire ever since her first album; however, the theme is not unique to her work. The style of the musical setting is not one of the most engaging or distinctive. That being said, "Bad Blood" was a major hit for Swift. In fact, in 2015 "Bad Blood" topped the Mainstream Top 40, the Hot 100 Airplay, the Hot Digital

Songs, and other charts. Not only was the video popular, but it also won the Grammy Award for Best Music Video.

Based on the fact that "Wildest Dreams," another Swift, Martin, Shellback collaborative composition, did not perform as well on the charts as "Bad Blood," it would appear that some listeners would disagree, but I prefer "Wildest Dreams." For one thing, this song contains more Swift signifiers than its predecessor. Specifically, the heavy use of the pentatonic scale in the melody and move between major and minor chords in the chorus are reminiscent of Swift's work going back to the very beginning of her career. Similarly, the reference to her character "standing in a nice dress" seems to reflect back to her "Tim McGraw" character wearing "that little black dress." The use of synthesizers and decidedly non-country-sounding drums and percussion programming clearly marks this as a product of Taylor Swift's mainstream pop period; however, there are sufficient connections to the older songs of Swift to satisfy both fans of the new and the old.

Swift, Martin, and Shellback also collaborated in writing "How You Get the Girl." Although tuneful and easily accessible on the surface, this is one of the more interesting tracks on *1989* in terms of its connections to the music of the decade of Taylor Swift's birth. The song opens with a repeated snippet of Swift's voice singing the pitch E, the tonic pitch of "How You Get the Girl." The sound, apparently sampled and sequenced, is actually reminiscent of the "ah, ah, ah" quarter-note iterations of a single-sampled pitch in Laurie Anderson's "O Superman," a song mentioned before in reference to the album. Programmers Martin and Shellback later turn the sample into a two-note figure, thereby moving more to the mainstream than had been the case in the early 1980s work by Anderson. In any case, listeners familiar with Laurie Anderson's work probably cannot help but suspect a connection between the two songs, especially given the stark similarity at the beginning of the Swift piece. Taylor Swift fans not familiar with the work of Laurie Anderson might interpret the repeated "ah" sample as the opening vocalization in Swift's "Mine" stripped to its bare essentials, to its most basic roots.

"How You Get the Girl" differs from quite a few of Swift's songs of loss in that in it she tells men how to repair broken relationships. Basically, her focus is on romance and humility. This is significant in that some of her earlier works ("Dear John" immediately comes to mind as an example) focused either on delivering angry accusations to her ex-lovers or on the pain she experienced when she was left or cheated on by her ex-lovers. It is as though her character has learned from experience and is eager to establish a lasting relationship herself and eager to spare other women the same heartache and angst that she experienced.

Also somewhat different than what might more typically had been the case for Swift earlier in her career is the fact that "How You Get the Girl" features a fairly large number of hard and soft rhymes in the verses. There are some typically Swiftian aspects of the song, though. One of the most notable is the melodic resemblance between the chorus and the chorus of "You Belong with Me." And although the phrase structure of the verses is most conventional than in some early Swift compositions, there are a couple of quirky extensions and elisions that are reminiscent of the somewhat outside-the-box approach to structure associated with Taylor Swift ever since her first album.

All in all, "How You Get the Girl" is an intriguing combination of the old and the new. The arrangement is not as thoroughly pop dance-oriented as some on *1989* but does include the heavy bass drum sound of modern 21st-century music, along with some interesting audio techniques that create a true sense of surprise the first time one hears the track. Specifically, coproducers Martin and Shellback cut off the natural reverberation of sound at several points. This somewhat disconcerting effect can cause listeners to question whether or not their headphones are plugged in all the way, or whether or not they have a loose speaker wire.

The next track on the album, "This Love," is a solo composition by Swift. It is also notable for the return of Swift's longtime producer and multi-instrumentalist Nathan Chapman, who was all but absent from producing and playing on *1989*. Although "This Love" does not represent a return to the country music that Swift and Chapman had created back in the first decade of the 21st century, the song is a gentle ballad, absent the thump-thump-thump of the percussion sequences that tend to dominate the album. In this song, Swift sings about a relationship that she had been in that has been rebuilt or rekindled. To put it another way, love does not leave Swift's character to be replaced with nothing more than regret, anger, resentment, and hurt. Here, she finds recovery and the return of love and the feeling of being in love. It is as though the song is a natural extension of the earlier track "How You Get the Girl." Lyrically, it is a pensive song, a mood song. The mood, the Zen-like state of being—or of needing to exist in this new-found state of happiness—is enhanced by an atmospheric musical setting, provided by coproducers Swift and Chapman, and a melody that is more organic and less goal-driven (toward a particular pitch, such as tonic) than many of Swift's tunes.

Clearly, early in her career Taylor Swift established herself as an autobiographical singer-songwriter. Conjuring up titles such as "Dear John" immediately after a highly publicized breakup with John Mayer and coding boys' names into the printed song lyrics in her CD booklets certainly confirmed Swift's reputation as a chronicler of her own relationships-gone-bad. As a result of this real and perceived focus, Swift and Ryan Tedder's creation of a song such as "I Know Places" might seem surprising to some fans. Here, Swift and Tedder create what sounds like a fantasy environment in which "they are the hunters; we are the foxes." The gist of the song is that the hunted animal—in this case Swift's character—knows hiding places in which the hunters (whether they be actual or metaphorical) cannot find her. The atmosphere created by the lyrics sounds as though it comes right out of a fantasy motion-picture soundtrack, more than something from another song by a confessional, relationship-driven, autobiographical constant loser at love, the unfortunate image with which some of Taylor Swift's early hits left her.

"I Know Places" reprises the opening sampled voice effect of "How You Get the Girl," except that this time the sampled and manipulated snippet is on the opening word of the song: "I." Coproducers Swift, Tedder, and Noel Zancanella turn the single pitch "I" into a two-pitch figure that drives the entire track. Although "I Know Places" incorporates the heavy and highly syncopated bass drum effect of 21st-century hip-hop, it is a tuneful and atmospheric song. As a result, this is one of the tracks on *1989* that reflects some of the old traits that originally made Swift a songwriting star, and it will not sound entirely foreign to the fans that she had had since her debut as a teenager.

The original release of *1989* concludes with "Clean," a song cowritten by Swift and Imogen Heap. At first glance, the combination of Swift and Heap might seem like an unlikely pairing. Certainly, the popular reception of the two with the music-buying public could not be much different: Swift hit the big time as a teenager and has not looked back, popularity speaking, while Heap's career has moved in fits and starts since just before the start of the 21st century. The result of this pairing, however, is one of the sleeper tracks on an album that was packed with hits. For one thing, Swift and Heap deal with a broken relationship using the metaphor of addiction, a new edgier, more mature-sounding reference point for Swift. The minimalistic percussion, keyboard, and programming by multi-instrumentalist Heap provide a nearly emotionless background for Swift's singing. The mood of the accompaniment goes a long way in painting Swift's character as someone so deeply wounded by the relationship that she has lost the ability to feel anything. Some of the specific references in the text, too, point to a hurt that defies any real sense of healing. Although the melody of the song is tuneful—creating appealing commercial music is a skill that Swift had perfected years before—Swift's performance is restrained and in character. One of the more interesting features of the song's construction is the approach of Swift and Heap to phrase structure. The song basically is built around four-measure units; however, in the verses the phrases are not balanced with respect to the amount of text in each. Although this does not go as far as some of Swift's earlier songs in creating a sense of extemporaneous expression, it provides enough of a jolt to force the listener to pay close attention to lyrics that are especially rich in imagery.

The "D.L.X.," or deluxe, edition of the CD release of *1989* includes bonus tracks, as one has come to expect from Big Machine Records' releases. One of the primary differences here is that the CD includes a couple of demo recordings that themselves offer the listener unexpected extras. Let us first take a look at the bonus studio tracks before examining the demos.

The first bonus track, "Wonderland," is a product of Swift, Max Martin, and Johan Shellback. The song's lyrical theme makes "Wonderland" seem perhaps more like a logical extension of the album *Red* than *1989*. Swift sings of falling into "Wonderland" with her lover, a state of being that she likens to falling "down the rabbit hole." The relationship is intense, dangerous. In short, it is a red-hot relationship destined to end in a crash-and-burn disaster, much like most of the relationships at the basis of *Red*. Musically, "Wonderland" is representative of Taylor Swift's move toward mainstream pop and dance-inspired music on both *Red* and *1989*. Structurally, the motivically based verse melody and more conventionally tuneful and gentle chorus fit into Swift's longtime tendency to provide a high degree of contrast between verses and chorus. However, Martin and Shellback bring the aggressive bass-drum effect of contemporary hip-hop and alternative rock into the mix.

"Wonderland" does not seem quite as organic as some of the best songs that appeared on the original versions of *Red* and *1989*. In particular, some listeners might find the sharpness of the contrast between the sections as too extreme. That being said, this contrast does match the bimodal nature of the relationship of which Swift sings. Throughout her career, Taylor Swift has written songs with asymmetrical phrase lengths—in general, she has never shied away from breaking out of the pop music conventions of four- and eight-measure phrases. In the chorus of "Wonderland," the last two words—"in Wonderland"—are extended. In fact, the end of the chorus sections seems to conclude in a sort of musical limbo before the next verse begins. Again, this can be understood as a musical manifestation of the relationship about which Swift sings; however, because the rest of the song emphasizes more clearly delineated phrases, Swift, Martin, and Shellback's approach to the chorus might not resonate with some listeners who prefer structural symmetry.

The ballad "You Are in Love," written by Swift and Jack Antonoff, is a track that illustrates the degree to which Swift was evolving as a lyricist in the second decade of the 21st century. In the verses, she presents a series of sometimes-disconnected and sometimes-connected images that illustrate various phases and various experiences in the ups and downs of a romantic relationship. Although some of Swift's earlier songs exhibited at least some degree of lyrical impressionism, impressionism rules the day in "You Are in Love" to the extent that the song clearly demonstrates that Swift was broadening her stylistic approach. Swift and Antonoff set these impressionistic images to a four-note motive that forms the melodic whole of each verse. It might logically be the highly repetitious nature of the verses that caused "You Are in Love" not to be included on the initial release of *1989*. The sense of timelessness, spaciousness, and almost emotional insecurity that comes from the repetitiveness of the verses, the atmospheric instrumental accompaniment, the cool unemotional vocal approach that Swift takes, and even the placement of the melodic motives low in Swift's vocal range all make for a song that deserves more than one listen. "You Are in Love" is not a conventional tuneful ballad, nor is it a catchy country-pop or pop-rock song like some of Swift's biggest-selling hits.

It is, instead, an example of a growing sophistication and a demonstration that an effective song need not necessarily push all the proverbial buttons for heavy airplay or single sales.

Although "You Are in Love" was almost anticommercial in style, the next bonus track, "New Romantics," was a successful commercial single by the time of the release of the "D.L.X," or deluxe, edition of the *1989* CD. Insofar as *1989* was inspired by the music of the decade of Taylor Swift's birth, "New Romantics" pretty clearly fits in with the group of songs included on the original running order of the album. One can hear elements of the expression of the coolness (or the hipness) of a generation of, say, the Bangles' "We Got the Beat" in "New Romantics." The sense of fashion that was at the core of new wave rock can clearly be seen in the characters that Swift counts among her cohort in this song. If one is looking for precedents for the characters of "New Romantics," though, one might also consider a song such as the Who's "My Generation." Not only are the members of Swift's generation cool and hip, they also exhibit signs of boredom and suffer from having (to paraphrase) "bricks thrown at them," characteristics of the Mods of the mid-1960s. Listeners might detect other possible inspirations in the lyrics of the song. Specifically, Swift and cowriters Max Martin and Shellback include some wordplay that suggests the work of Elvis Costello. Listeners familiar with the work of both Swift and Costello might make an immediate connection between Costello's pun "there's no such thing as an original sin" and Swift's pun "the best people in life are free." The problem with wordplay such as this—as there are elements of this in other songs that were on the original release of *1989*—is that one listener's clever wordplay is another listener's glib use of clichés. Despite the apparent ties to the new wave rock era, musically "New Romantics" is more about the pop music of the 21st century than about the prevailing styles of the late 1970s and early 1980s.

One of the most notable features of the "D.L.X." edition of *1989* is the approach taken by Big Machine Records and coexecutive producers Swift and Max Martin to the demos. In Swift's spoken introduction to the demo version of "I Know Places," she explains that the demos were selected to illustrate her approach to songwriting, from the initial conception of the song to the finished product. This aligns with what Swift has been doing in recent years with her videos: providing documentaries about the making of the videos, thus providing her fans with an insider's view of the creative process.

Swift opens her discussion of the genesis of "I Know Places" by telling the listener that she sometimes begins with lyrics, sometimes with the music, and works in different ways, depending on the song. She then states that for "I Know Places" she sent a piano/vocal demo to collaborator Ryan Tedder the night before they completed and recorded the song. Swift used her phone to record her singing and playing and to send the demo in the form of a voice memo to Tedder.[9] Swift's piano accompaniment is minimalist and consists of half-note arpeggios during the verses and a largely homophonic block-chord-plus-bass-note texture during the chorus. Still, the basic ideas (lyrics, harmony, melody, tempo, and mood) of the song are in place on the demo. Interestingly, the "I, I, I, I" figure that sounds like it could have been created electronically from a sample on the finished recording is included in Swift's acoustic rendition of the song.

In the introduction to the demo version of Swift's collaboration with her friend Jack Antonoff, "I Wish You Would," Swift identifies the song as an example of one of her more recent songwriting techniques. She goes on to describe "hanging out" with Antonoff, who shared an instrumental track that he had stored on his phone. Swift describes the guitar sounds as "amazing" and states that she asked Antonoff on the spot if she could have the track because she immediately could imagine a finished song based on it. After Antonoff sent Swift the track, she recorded her working vocal part on her phone, singing to the Antonoff-supplied track that was on Swift's laptop computer.[10]

Swift explains that she introduced her phone-recorded demo of the song "Blank Space" to her collaborators Max Martin and Johan Shellback in the recording studio. She tells the listener that when she, Martin, and Shellback collaborate, they keep a phone recording the entire time, in case someone "blurts out an idea" that the three later want to incorporate into the finished song.[11] The version of the "Blank Space" demo included on the special edition of *1989* consists of Swift's introduction of the song to her two collaborators. Indeed, as Swift had earlier described, as she, Martin, and Shellback listen to Swift's vocal and guitar version of the song, Martin and Shellback improvise backing vocal figures that eventually became part of the finished arrangement of the song that was recorded in the studio.

Big Machine Records' packaging of *1989* reached a peak in offering Taylor Swift's fans added value. Not only does the package include a booklet with all song lyrics and performance and production credits, it also contains an enclosed sleeve with photographs of Swift that appears to be designed to look as though it were a personal gift from Swift to the consumer. This marketing approach is consistent with the way in which the demos on the special edition of the album gives Taylor Swift's fans a sort of insider's view into various aspects of her songwriting process and her relationship with her cowriters.

It is important to note that after years of having others serve as "executive producers" of her albums, Taylor Swift shared that duty with Max Martin on *1989*. This suggests the growing level of control that Swift had over her finished product in the middle of the 2010s, especially compared with her first several albums, on which she received little to no production credit. Various interviews, video documentaries, and the like all suggest that Swift has had a strong well-developed vision for her projects even going back several years before the recording of *1989*. Now that vision and its fruition seem to have been formalized.

Undoubtedly, some fans of Swift's early country style were surprised and perhaps even disappointed by the musical styles that Swift and her cowriters and coproducers integrated into *1989*. Generally, critical reception to *1989* was not quite as favorable as had been the case with *Fearless*. Some critics did, however, embrace Swift's increased lyrical sophistication, including *Billboard*'s Jem Aswad.[12] Despite less-than-unanimous approval from fans and critics, *1989* was a strong commercial success and was well received by members of the Recording Academy, the organization that honors artists with the Grammys. In 2015, *1989* received a Grammy for Album of the Year and Best Pop Vocal Album, and the track "Bad Blood" won the Grammy for Best Music Video. In addition, *1989* topped the pop album charts in several countries, and the singles "Shake It Off," "Wildest Dreams," "Style," "Blank Space," and "Bad Blood" were all significant commercial hits. In fact, the fact that *1989* spent over an entire year in the *Billboard* 200 and sold as well as it did put it in the same company as massive commercial successes of the past such as Fleetwood Mac's *Rumours*, Bruce Springsteen's *Born in the U.S.A.*, and Celine Dion's *Falling into You*.[13] Interestingly, throughout 2015 and 2016, Big Machine Records continued to release new singles and music videos related to *1989* (either the original version or one of the special editions), including videos for "Out of the Woods" and "New Romantics." Through these releases and through the continuing presence of *1989* on the charts, this album seems to be destined to become one of the best-selling albums by a female artist in the history of the recording industry.

Beyond Music

Not all popular music stars successfully make forays into the world of television, theater, or film; however, it can be argued that some of the biggest stars from the 20th century to the present have successfully crossed over between different media, often with success in one medium feeding success in another. Taylor Swift has not developed a film or a television presence to the extent of some other popular musicians of her generation; however, she has made some forays into other media that deserve mention.

Perhaps Swift's earliest significant not-entirely-musical performance on television was her January 2009 hosting of the popular NBC program *Saturday Night Live*. As *Billboard*'s Erin Strecker pointed out in her January 2015 article "Remember When Taylor Swift Shined As *Saturday Night Live* Host?" Swift hosted the program before the huge Grammy-winning success of *Fearless* and well before the enormity of her crossover appeal had realized its commercial potential. Still, as Strecker points out, Swift took to the television medium like a natural.[1]

Later in 2009, Swift made a cameo appearance as herself in the Disney film *Hannah Montana: The Movie*. This was an especially interesting venue for a Swift performance, as in some respects the real-life story of young Taylor Swift bears at least some resemblance to the fictional story of Miley Stewart and her alter ego Hannah Montana, played by Miley Cyrus. Interestingly, *Hannah Montana: The Movie* deals with the Stewart/Montana character trying to reconcile her real life as an average American rural teenager and her secret life as a country music star. Swift, even in many of her early songs, dealt with issues of identity and authenticity in one's life, and, especially in her soon-to-be-released and much-heralded *Fearless*, which dealt with these issues in the context of American high schools, a Hannah Montana-type of milieu.

Significantly, Swift's performance of her own composition, "Crazier," in *Hannah Montana: The Movie* has been acknowledged by at least some critics as perhaps the musical highlight of the film—despite the fact that the film includes a generous amount of music, both performed by its star, Miley Cyrus, and by others. For example, according to All Music Guide's critic Heather Phares, "... the best song on *Hannah Montana: The Movie* belongs to Taylor Swift. Her 'Crazier' is more genuine, more effortless, than any of Miley or Hannah's tracks, which is all the more interesting considering that Swift is, in a lot of ways, what Hannah Montana was aiming for in the first place: a massive teen star with country roots and pop polish who seems comfortable in, and delivers the best of, both of those worlds."[2] The song, a collaborative effort of Swift and Robert Ellis Orrall, is about the experience of falling in love. As Swift and Orrall relate the experience, this relationship seems to bear more than a passing resemblance to the red-hot relationships that would later form the basis of Swift's album *Red*. The key to this is Swift's description of falling and the "crazier" feeling that it imparts. This is a dangerous sort of love, the kind that in many Taylor Swift songs ends in disaster. The outcome of the relationship, however, is not part of this song. The song, in fact, plays an important role as part of the storyline of the movie and a relationship in which Stewart/Montana is involved. The other song that Swift wrote for *Hannah Montana: The Movie*, "You'll Always Find Your Way Back Home," will be detailed in Chapter 6, "The Singer or the Song?" as it is a vehicle for the Hannah Montana character.

The year 2009 included other Taylor Swift appearances. One of the more intriguing was her performance as an actor in the *CSI: Crime Scene Investigation* episode "Turn, Turn, Turn," which originally aired in March 2009. In this episode, Swift portrayed a troubled teen who (spoiler alert) ultimately was stabbed and killed with scissors by her overly controlling mother. Unlike her primarily comic appearance on *Saturday Night Live* and her cameo as herself in *Hannah Montana: The Movie*, here Swift had to play a decidedly un-Taylor Swift-like character. The role also required an emotional range that extended well beyond her other work as an actor during this period. The *CSI* episode also included Swift's song "You're Not Sorry" in a hip-hop-inspired remix, a stark stylistic contrast to the arrangement of the song that appeared on Swift's *Fearless*. Interestingly, the *CSI* remix of "You're Not Sorry" sounds very much like the musical direction that Swift took in some of the songs on her 2012 album *Red* and even more fully on her 2014 album, *1989*. However, the stylistic character of the "You're Not Sorry" remix probably has less to do with it being some sort of harbinger of Swift's own musical progression several years out, as it does with serving as a musical representation of the character that Swift portrayed in the television program.

It is probably fortunate for Taylor Swift's acting career, should she pursue it more actively in the future, that she appeared in *CSI: Crime Scene*

Investigation as early as she did, particularly because of the fact that she portrayed a character apparently so unlike herself and because the role required a variety of emotions. Swift's next major appearance was in a perhaps less artistically satisfying role, as a stereotypical high school ditz in the 2010 movie *Valentine's Day*. It was here that Swift first worked with the actor Taylor Lautner—the two played high school sweethearts who agreed to wait to have sex with each other, even while the friend of Swift's character planned her first sexual experience with her boyfriend. Lautner and Swift were romantically involved briefly. Although *Valentine's Day* included Swift's song "Today Was a Fairytale," which was a massive sales hit, Swift's character seems like a caricature, especially compared to the character she portrayed in *CSI* the previous year.

In addition to these and other sporadic film and television appearances and her numerous music videos, Swift has appeared in a number of documentaries. Some of her documentary work was captured in a three-part miniseries on the children's television network, The Hub. In addition, several of the special editions of Swift's albums include documentaries about the making of some of Swift's music videos. The reason I mention these appearances here is that in them, Swift exhibits a naturalness for the medium, especially as she explains the process of preparing for and shooting the videos. She comes across as a celebrity who not only appears in music videos but also one who understands the processes involved.

As mentioned earlier, Swift has appeared in a fair number of music videos. The videos for "You Belong with Me" and "Mean" are especially memorable, particularly as examples of Swift's early work. And, it is the video for "Mean," probably more than the song itself, that helped to make this song an anthem for diversity, for the underdog, and against bullying. The official video for her 2014 song "Bad Blood" earned Swift the 2016 Grammy for Best Music Video. Not all of Swift's music videos, however, have met with universal acclaim. The video for "Wildest Dreams" was based on classic Hollywood films set in Africa, such as *The Africa Queen* and *Out of Africa*. "Wildest Dreams" came under some fire for its all-white cast (the actors in the Hollywood classic-style movie that Swift appears to be making in the video as well as the actors who portray members of the film crew like the director, cameraman, and others). Joseph Kahn, the video's director, defended the casting as reflective of the casting in mid-20th-century Hollywood films set in Africa as well as the realities of the demographics of the Hollywood film crews of the period.[3]

The Singer or the Song?

When considering the career of Taylor Swift, it is important to remember that she gained local, regional, and eventually national recognition as a singer. Swift's family, however, moved from Pennsylvania to Tennessee so that Swift might stand a better chance at being signed as a songwriter. Many of the songs on the 16-year-old Swift's debut album seem to come from the viewpoint of an older woman. "Cold as You," for example, suggests a world-weariness that sounds as though it may have come out a marriage in which the husband's emotional connection to his wife had gradually faded away. To put it another way, "Cold as You" seems more like a song that might have been written with a Nashville-style Tin Pan Alley desire to shop around to established female country singing stars, as opposed to a song that was matched to the life experiences of a 16-year-old. Many other Swift songs, especially those written after her debut album, are clearly autobiographical. Still, Swift has written some songs for other performers, and some recording artists have covered Swift's songs, even those that seem to be clearly autobiographical. This begs the question: Is Taylor Swift a success because of her work as a singer, or because of her work as songwriter? Let us consider some of the songs that Swift has written for others as well as a few of the successful covers of Swift's compositions.

Certainly, one must consider "You'll Always Find Your Way Back Home," which Swift and Martin Johnson wrote for country singer/actress Miley Cyrus to sing in *Hannah Montana: The Movie*. Interestingly, structurally the song is not all that different than some of the songs that Cyrus had performed as Montana in the *Hannah Montana* television series. For example, the 2007

Hannah Montana song "Nobody's Perfect" is similarly built from short motives. What perhaps is most interesting about Swift and Johnson's vehicle for the Hannah Montana character in the movie is that it is more in the country-pop style than some of the more dance-oriented, synthesizer-driven songs (e.g., the aforementioned "Nobody's Perfect") that Miley Cyrus sang as the Montana character in the television series. In the context of the film's narrative, this is significant, as the movie deals primarily with the Stewart/Montana character's pull between living a simple, rural, country lifestyle and the fast-paced life of stardom in California. Swift and Johnson's up-tempo country-pop song manages to allow the film's character to exist in both worlds simultaneously. That being said, it is important to note that the country-rock style of "You'll Always Find Your Way Back Home" is entirely consistent with Swift's compositions written for her own use. In the context of Taylor Swift's compositions of the time period, however, the extensive use of short melodic motives in the chorus is unusual. It was more common for Swift to balance the motivically oriented melodies of many of her verses with higher-register and more tuneful chorus melodies in the works that Swift wrote for herself.

The lyrical focus on things that one might wish to change in one's life in "You'll Always Find Your Way Back Home" is also consistent with the themes that Swift explores in songs written for her own use; however, the themes extend beyond typical Swiftian situations, thus suggesting the ties of the song to the storyline in *Hannah Montana: The Movie*. Interestingly, the lyrical focus on ties to home works not only in the context of the film, in which Miley Cyrus's character, Miley Stewart/Hannah Montana is torn between her rural country roots and the pop music stardom in Hollywood, but also in the broader context of the continuum of country music going all the way back to the genre's first superstar singer-songwriter, Jimmie Rodgers. Specifically, in songs such as "Daddy and Home," to cite just one example, Rodgers explored the bimodality of his character's life, a life in which he is torn between the desire "to roam" (and all that might imply) and the desire to be back home with his ailing father.

One of the more interesting projects involving other artists covering Taylor Swift's songs is Ryan Adams's September 2015 release of *1989*, which included rock versions of the entire Swift album. In the hands of Adams, "Welcome to New York" sounds remarkably like a mid-1980s Bruce Springsteen arrangement, just absent Clarence Clemons's tenor saxophone. In fact, the spirit of Springsteen when he was at his peak of popularity runs through several tracks on *1989*. One of the more surprisingly effective songs is the Adams arrangement and performance of "Shake It Off," in which Adams adopts a Springsteen-like emotionally drained–sounding vocal style in a musical arrangement that sounds like those of Springsteen's "I'm on Fire." Adams uses an acoustic focus on "Blank Space." In fact, it can be argued that Adams's version of "Blank Space" is more personal and less tied to the stylistic trends of any given decade than Swift's hip-hop-inspired version of her composition. Although I will not detail all of the tracks on the Ryan Adams *1989* album, suffice it to say that Adams's arrangements, tempos, and vocal style contrast in some cases quite widely with those of Taylor Swift. All in all, though, Adams's adaptations of Swift's songs work very well. Although undoubtedly part of the credit for this goes to Adams for devising treatments that complement Swift's words, melodies, and harmonies, the success of the Adams album also demonstrates that Taylor Swift's compositions are strong enough to succeed in a variety of versions. This may come as a surprise to listeners who consider some of the Swift's verse melodies to be too heavily based on short motives—especially the more repetitious verse melodies—however, they work beautifully in the hands of Adams. In fact, the melodic simplicity of some of the verses combined with the large amount of text in some of Swift's songs actually lends itself well to the acoustic treatment that Adams gives to pieces such as "Shake It Off" and "Blank Space." These songs sound like they were fully intended to be confessional singer-songwriter-style pieces. It should be noted that Adams released "Bad Blood" as a single prior to releasing the *1989* album. Interestingly, Taylor Swift named the Adams interpretation of "Bad Blood" as one of her favorite covers in a *Billboard* article that appeared before the release of Adams's album.[1]

Also notable in Swift's list of favorite covers are versions of "Shake It Off" by Tenor Buds, Labrinth, Jesse Will, and Kelly Clarkson.[2] Interestingly, these versions include adaptations of Swift's hit song into reggae, ballad, and other stylistic feels. Again, as is the case with Ryan Adams's singer-songwriter style adaptation of the song, the variety of ways in which artists have treated "Shake It Off" suggests the strength of the words and music (absent the arrangement).

For Taylor Swift fans, the year 2016 probably brought much disappointment. Sure, Swift was in the news—if for nothing else than a highly publicized tiff with Kanye West and Kim Kardashian[3]—and Swift gave several notable, high-profile performances. She did not, however, release any new material in 2016. Why was this so important? Swift had established a pattern early in her career of releasing a new album every two years, and in even-numbered years, in fact. As a songwriter, Swift was active, however. She provided the song "This Is What You Came For" for her ex-boyfriend Calvin Harris, who collaborated on his recording with Rihanna. Swift also wrote "Better Man" for the group Little Big Town. Interestingly, Swift's identity as the writer of the two songs was masked by the performers and their record companies. In the case of the Harris/Rihanna recording, Swift was given an assumed name, and in the case of the Little Big Town recording, Swift was not identified by name until "nearly two weeks after its release," according to Elias Leight of *Billboard* magazine.[4] Leight's brief article about Swift's stealthy songwriting contributions of 2016 includes analysis from songwriter Busbee about Swift's work. According to Busbee, "This Is What You Came For" "is the truest pop song in her [Swift's] catalog in the modern sense: it's just an emotion."[5] Taylor Swift's work as a provider of songs to other performers brings us back to the reason that she and her family moved to Nashville when Swift was a teenager so that she might better enter the Nashville scene as a professional songwriter. Time will only tell, but given the slow pace with which she has released new albums and singles as a performer, and given her recent work as a songwriter for others, perhaps that is the direction in which Swift will move in the future.

Unlike some other singer-songwriters, Taylor Swift has released precious few recordings of material by other songwriters. In fact, with the exception of her early Christmas EP, *The Taylor Swift Holiday Collection*, Swift's performances and recordings of songs composed by other writers have been more like one-off occurrences. As a result, it is difficult to determine how much of Swift's appeal is solely related to her work as a singer. Had Swift made hit recordings of others' songs—such as, say, James Taylor, whose biggest-selling singles and perhaps most iconic recordings ironically have been songs written by others (e.g., "How Sweet It Is (To Be Loved By You)" and "You've Got a Friend"), it might be easier to separate out Swift's connection with her audience between her words and music, on one hand, and her singing, on the other hand. As Swift's career stands at this time, it seems to be safe to say that the successful covers of her material suggests the strength of her songs outside of the context of Swift-as-performer; however, the heavily autobiographical nature of Swift's work and the apparently intense interest that Swift's fans have in the connections of her work to her private life suggest that Taylor Swift is one singer-songwriter for whom it might always be particularly difficult to separate the singer from the song.

Conclusions: A Woman of Her Time

7

Undoubtedly, a major reason that Taylor Swift deserves a lasting place in the story of American popular music is based on her critical and, especially, commercial success. To date, Swift is the only female performer to have won multiple Grammys for Album of the Year, and those albums that won that coveted award also won in other categories. Swift has been called by at least one music critic "the voice of her generation,"[1] and importantly, her generation and the entire world have been witness to her artistic and personal growth from being a teenaged country singing and songwriting prodigy to a mature singer-songwriter eager to take on virtually any genre or combination of genres. Every one of Taylor Swift's albums has topped either the country charts or the pop charts, and several topped both. In addition, Swift's albums have demonstrated the kind of chart longevity that places them in the same company as the sales-leading classics of the past. In today's age of downloads, Swift's physical albums, in the form of the original CDs and the special edition reissues that have appeared shortly after the originals, have sold unusually well. This suggests that music fans prefer owning something tangible and longer lasting from her than the more transitory electronic files that they might purchase of other artists. And, although it can be argued that Taylor Swift is primarily an album-oriented artist, every one of her albums to date has contained multiple charting—and sometimes multiple chart-topping—singles. Irrespective of the sales and critical success, Swift is acknowledged and respected among musicians—even those who are not necessarily fans—as one highly successful artist who actually writes her own songs and almost exclusively performs solely her own material.

There is, however, much more to the story of the importance of Taylor Swift and her work. Swift's use of social media reflects the changing nature of the media with which she maintains contact with her fans, previews new material, carries on the occasional public tiff with other celebrities (and ex-boyfriends), and generally maintains visibility with the public when she does not have a brand-new album on the charts. Swift has also exhibited a new type of feminism that is recognized as a message of empowerment by some women of her generation but is considerably more controversial among some feminists of the past. This reflects the generational battle that emerged in feminists' perspectives of the Hillary Clinton versus Bernie Sanders battle for the Democratic nomination in the 2016 presidential campaign cycle. Primarily in the second decade of the 21st century, Taylor Swift has been a vocal advocate for the rights of songwriters and performers, particularly revolving the dissemination of their work via streaming media outlets such as Spotify and iTunes Radio. We will now examine in more detail each of these aspects of Swift's work.

SOCIAL MEDIA AND TECHNOLOGY

Over the course of her career, Taylor Swift has defied the more traditional paths of other singer-songwriters. If she had not, she would not have been a professional Nashville writer before she was old enough to drive a car. Part of Swift's career has involved the use of social media in building a fan base, maintaining connections with fans, selling her music, and so on. Interestingly, in the second decade of the 21st century, Swift has also generated coverage in the entertainment industry press for other uses of technology. Although Swift certainly is not alone in her use of modern technology, her prominence in the music industry and the fact that she has remained current with technology make Taylor Swift an example of what is going on in the world of the intersections of popular entertainment and technology that is available to the masses.

Early on in Taylor Swift's career, she made notable use of social media. Swift promoted her debut single, "Tim McGraw," using MySpace. At the time—2006—MySpace was reputed to be the largest social networking site in the world. It was also especially popular with high school–aged Americans—Taylor Swift's demographic at the time. Interestingly, the industry press and radio industry insiders took notice of Swift's use of MySpace in promoting "Tim McGraw" and other early work. For example, Katie Hasty's 2007 article on the start of Swift's career in *Billboard* quotes Becky Brenner, program director of the Seattle, Washington, country radio station KMPS-FM, as acknowledging that Swift's use of MySpace played an important role in bringing "Tim McGraw" not only to the attention of Swift's early fan base but also to radio disc jockeys.[2]

MySpace still exists, but over the years, the demographics of users of social media platforms have evolved, and, obviously, Taylor Swift has matured beyond her teenaged years. In fact, as Swift grew older and Facebook increasingly became the dominant social media outlet for her generation, Swift used Facebook as a platform to connect with her fans and to promote her recordings and live appearances. She continued to ride the technological wave by later turning to Twitter and tweeting on a regular basis; she later became a user of Instagram and Tumblr. Each of these shifts has roughly coincided to nationwide trends in the use of social media. Although Swift's evolution in this regard reflects the changes that have occurred within her generation in terms of preferred social media outlets, it is important to note that Swift has not abandoned the social media platforms of the past as she has ventured into Instagram, Tumblr, and so forth: she still has a presence on Facebook, for example. As a result, a Taylor Swift fan need not be entirely up to date on the latest flashy and trendy social media application out there in order to maintain a connection with his or her favorite singer-songwriter.

Swift's addition—as opposed to replacement—of social media platforms seems to align with her intergenerational popularity. In fact, members of the media have made it a point to note the intergenerational nature of the appeal of Swift's music. For example, *Billboard* writer Tom Roland noted this aspect of Taylor Swift's fan base in his October 23, 2010, article "Princess Superstar."[3] Interestingly, Louis Hau, Ed Christman, and Craig Marks, writing in the same magazine, noted the same attribute in their much shorter November 13, 2010, article "The Only Girl in the World."[4]

Celebrities' use of social media has not solely involved the development and maintenance of a fan base. In recent years, a number of entertainment personalities have squared off against each other through social media platforms such as Facebook and Twitter. Some of these celebrity spats have been long lasting and highly publicized. Taylor Swift was not entirely immune to this aspect of the use of social media. In one fairly short-lived spat, singer Niki Minaj squared off on social media over Swift's nomination for an MTV VMA award for the "Bad Blood" video. Minaj was not nominated for an award and in a tweet implied that only videos that featured slim women were nominated. Many fans, and apparently Swift herself, took this as a stab at Swift for her nominated video. Although the series of tweets between the artists was brief, this incident is indicative of how even the briefest of public social media conflicts of this sort can generate media attention.[5] More recently, throughout 2016, Swift has engaged in a battle in social media and in the electronic media of Internet entertainment sites and television with celebrity Kim Kardashian and her husband rapper Kanye West, the man who continues to claim that his interruption of Swift's acceptance speech at the 2009 Video Music Awards ceremony was largely—if not solely—responsible for making Swift famous.[6] Interestingly, at the same time that Kardashian, West, and Swift were publicly sparring, the *Journal of Popular Music Studies* published a lengthy study of the racial/sociological dynamics surrounding West's interruption of Swift's acceptance speech back in 2009.[7]

The continuing importance of social media exposure for Taylor Swift as a celebrity is confirmed by the results of her posting of photographs of herself and her then boyfriend Calvin Harris on Instagram in March 2016. According to an article by Emily White of *Billboard*, the Instagram posting helped Swift to jump from No. 13 to No. 4 on the "Social 50" chart and helped Harris to reenter the chart at No. 14. White also mentions that according to Next Big Sound, "Swift tallied a 282% gain in reactions on Instagram" after her posting of the Swift-Harris vacation photos.[8]

Over the years, Swift has used and continues to use various other electronic applications to keep in touch with fans and ill children with special requests. For example, in 2015, Swift used FaceTime to talk with a terminally ill 4-year-old.[9] Although the jaded individual might point out that Swift received a degree of favorable publicity from talking with the young fan, Swift seems to give of her time in situations such as this to a greater extent than some other celebrities and uses a wide variety of forums (e.g., in-person visits, FaceTime, social media) to interact with fans who are in special need of her encouragement.

More recently, in July 2016, Swift met with children suffering with cancer at Lady Cilento Children's Hospital in Brisbane, Australia. Swift and the patients took and posted selfies on Twitter and Instagram, which were instantly seen and commented on around the world.[10]

Swift's use of FaceTime to connect with one particular fan and her snapping and posting selfies with children in Australia are not the only examples of how she has either met with and given encouragement to seriously ill children and adults. In some cases, social media coverage of a fan's need or request has precipitated Swift's response. Interestingly, this calls to mind the findings of sociologist David Beer as expressed in his article "Making Friends with Jarvis Cocker: Music Culture in the Context of Web 2.0." In the article, Beer discusses the extent to which social media appears to bring down the wall or perception of "distance between popstar and interested enthusiast."[11] In the case of Swift's apparent responses to fans' posts, tweets, and so on—as publicly shown by her personal appearances and FaceTime conversations—Swift demonstrates enough of a connection to her fans through social media that at least distance between them and Swift appears to be bridged by the various media.

As Microsoft Research's Nancy K. Baym wrote in her paper "Fans or Friends?: Seeing Social Media Audiences As Musicians Do," by the start of the second decade of the 21st century "nearly all music professionals seem convinced that social media—and in particular musicians' use of those media to connect with audiences—are key to their survival."[12] Taylor Swift seems to have recognized this even as she was using social media to start her recording career a good four to five years before the time period when there was widespread acknowledgment of how crucial the use of social media is for the 21st-century popular musician.

Although the details of the artists' connections with a strongly loyal fan base differ considerably, the use of social media as a means to gather together a disparate group of fans used by Lady Gaga and Taylor Swift bears some resemblance. Writing in *Popular Music and Society*, Melissa Click, Hyunji Lee, and Holly Willson Holladay detail how Lady Gaga has used social media as a means of empowering young fans who had felt like outsiders and who had been bullied.[13] Swift's connections with her young fans may not have resulted in a subculture of "Monsters," Lady Gaga's newly empowered fans, but it does appear that both artists have used social media to help their fans have a shared vision. In both cases, the tight connection of fans to their favorite artists suggests the extent to which social media has gone far, far beyond the fan clubs of earlier generations of pop musicians and fans.

Taylor Swift's association with 21st-century technology that is available to and used by the masses does not solely come in the form of her use of social media. Swift is one of a group of relatively young singer-songwriters who makes use of the music-creation possibilities offered by portable devices such as smartphones, tablets, and laptop computers. The "D.L.X." or deluxe CD edition of *1989* contains the usual bonus tracks; however, the album also includes demo versions of "I Wish You Would," "I Know Places," and "Blank Space." What is most fascinating about these tracks is that Swift provides a spoken introduction to each demo version and describes how each represents her approach to songwriting. Interestingly, Swift discusses how she uses her smartphone as a musical note-taking device, both in her solo demos and in her collaborations with musicians such as Jack Antonoff, Max Martin, and Johan Shellback. In the pop song compositional world of Taylor Swift, the smartphone helps the songwriter keep fragments of songs, share partial or complete backing tracks across the world, and so on. Although Swift focuses on her work in this manner with her immediate collaborators, they are not alone in using the voice memo software built into devices such as Apple's iPhone. App developers have since taken the idea of the voice memos one step farther. Not only post-*1989* products such as Apple's Music Memos as well as similar products by other third-party developers allow musicians to record their works in progress, but also some of the apps will detect rhythmic, melodic, and harmonic patterns and automatically add drums, bass, and other accompaniment to the recording. In fact, some press coverage of those new apps included information about Swift's use of the Voice Memos.[14]

EMPOWERMENT AND FEMINISM

Throughout her career, Taylor Swift has been seen as a supporter of the underdog, the bullied, and those who do not necessarily appear to live up to conventional society's expectations. As detailed in previous chapters, Swift's album *Fearless* revolved around the high school travails of the students who do not fit in with the cool kids. The distinction between those who are in and those who are out might be even more dramatically drawn in the album's booklet or in the music videos than in the lyrics of the songs themselves.

For example, the video for "You Belong with Me" draws a clear distinction between Swift's character (tee shirt and glasses, playing clarinet in the marching band, etc.) and her rival (short skirts, no glasses, cheerleader, actively seeking the football star's attention, etc.). And just what is the message of empowerment in this video? Ultimately, it is Swift's character that ends up with the football star at the prom. Her naturalness and sincerity win the day over the more calculated and self-serving ways of her rival. Swift's slightly later song "Mean" appears to be directed at a music critic who dismissed Swift's singing ability, with the song's lyrics making it clear that the character to whom Swift sings has in the past told her that "[she] can't sing." The music video, however, is framed around a number of characters who are bullied, but who by the end of the video end up attaining their dreams: the young man who reads fashion magazines ends up as a fashion designer, the girl who does not fit in with the cool kids gets her college diploma, and so on. Still later, Swift's "Welcome to New York" presents listeners with a New York City in which "you can want who you want, boys and boys, and girls and girls." These lyrics were understood as a statement of at least acceptance, if not empowerment, by some members of the LGBTQ community.

Swift's expressions of empowerment have not been limited to her songs. Swift has used the various platforms with which she has been afforded through her success as a singer-songwriter to champion women's rights and artists' rights. And as winner of Grammys, Video Music Association (VMA) Awards, and Country Music Television (CMT) Awards, Swift has had ample opportunities to make public statements on these issues. For example, at the 2016 Grammy Awards ceremony, Swift warned female artists to make sure that they allow no one to undercut them or to take credit for their work.[15]

Taylor Swift has also put her money where her mouth is, to use an old saw. For example, in February 2016, Swift donated $250,000 to the singer Kesha. Kesha had lodged a lawsuit in 2014 against her then producer Dr. Luke alleging sexual and other abuse. Kesha subsequently sued Sony to be released from her contract with the company and Dr. Luke. Although the totality of the legal action in the case is ongoing, in February 2016 a court ruled against nullifying Kesha's contract with the recording company. Swift made her donation to Kesha to help with the singer's legal expenses. Because of the nature of Kesha's complaint against Dr. Luke, fans interpreted Swift's donation of $250,000 as an act of feminism.

It should also be noted that Taylor's Swift's philanthropic gifts have not just benefited individual fans or fellow artists such as Kesha. On August 17, 2016, Swift announced that she would be donating $1 million toward flood relief in Louisiana. Swift thanked the fans of the state for their kindness when she opened the U.S. leg of her *1989* World Tour in 2015.[16]

Interestingly, early in the 2010s, there was public debate in the press and electronic media about Swift's music, her public persona, her public statements and actions, and what they represented vis-à-vis female empowerment and feminism. The contrasting viewpoints of Swift can be observed by comparing the article "Swift Judgment: Who Made Taylor Swift the Sex Police?" written by Rachel McCarthy James and published in the Spring 2011 issue of *Bitch Magazine: Feminist Response to Pop Culture*, with a subsequent letter to the editor to the same magazine by Taylor Swift's fan Lora Zorian, who was a reader of the magazine.[17] In alignment with Rachel McCarthy James's dismissal of what some Swift fans interpret as feminism, Janet Albrechtsen's article "The Corruption of Feminism" in the Winter 2015 issue of *Policy* described the brand of feminism associated with Swift and actress Gwyneth Paltrow as "corrupt."[18]

Interestingly, the comparison of these articles with the response of *Bitch Magazine* reader Lora Zorian seems to parallel the debate that was ongoing in early 2016 regarding the challenges that the Hillary Clinton campaign was having with drumming up support from young women (who saw Bernie Sanders as the more empowering of the two Democratic candidates), despite the strong support of longtime well-established feminist personalities such as Gloria Steinem and Madeleine Albright. The assessment of Swift seems to draw similar battle lines between the 1970s view of feminism and how young women of Swift's generation view and interpret "feminism" and "female empowerment."

This battle between the generations has resulted in numerous blog posts and opinion-editorial (op-ed) pieces in a variety of media. One particularly interesting op-ed piece was written by 18-year-old Taylor Vidmar and published by MTV News. As Vidmar puts it, "Ironically, these reeking-of-the-patriarchy statements [Steinem and Albright's statements rather strong declarations that true feminists could not support Sanders, a man, against Clinton, a woman] directly exemplify the irrelevance and hypocrisy young feminists like myself want to avoid. Many older feminists seem to be unaware of the intersectional feminism of today, which is focused more than ever on issues like race, religion, and sexuality, among so many others."[19] Swift's songs and her public statements of empowerment, although not necessarily dealing with race and religion per se, do seem to align with the "intersectional feminism" of which Vidmar wrote. In particular, Swift has taken on bullying as a focal point, particularly in the video for "Mean" and throughout *Fearless*.

Perhaps less controversial—and almost certainly less apparently tied to generational differences in how one defines "empowerment"—is Swift's very public defense of artists' rights, particularly as they intersect with new technologies. Swift took on Apple after the computer giant announced that it would not pay artists' royalties on songs that were provided to listeners for free during the Apple Music streaming audio service's trial period. Swift published an open letter to Apple on the Internet, using Tumblr to deliver her post. In the words of 21st-century Internet vernacular, Swift's Tumblr post went viral. In the estimation of *Time*'s Tim Bajarin, Swift's use of social media as a form of social protest caused Apple to do what the business world considered completely unexpected: "change its mind."[20] Speaking of *Time*, Swift's influence over Apple was duly noted by numerous popular media sources, so noteworthy and so demonstrative of the power of Swift in the world of popular culture. *Time* ran several print and Internet-based articles about the brief Swift-Apple standoff, as did the *Christian Science Monitor* and other popular press and media outlets.[21]

In addition to Apple Music, Swift took on the streaming audio service Spotify in 2014. She pulled her music from the service, citing what she viewed as low payment of royalties to artists. Interestingly, at the time Swift told the press that she bought digital music by new, emerging performers on Apple's iTunes.[22] As would be the case two years later when Swift took on Apple Music, the media noted that perhaps Swift alone could pull her music from Spotify because, in the words of *Time*'s Victor Luckerson, "she operates on a different plan from the rest of the music biz."[23]

When studying Swift's relationship with streaming audio providers, it is interesting to note that her pulling of her music from Spotify occurred at a time in which younger music fans were moving away from services such as Pandora to newer services such as Spotify. Statista.com states that "in 2015, [Pandora] was most popular among users aged 35 to 44 and 18 to 24."[24] Although Taylor Swift did not fall directly into either of those categories, being in the 25–26 range, one could reasonably assume that a hefty number of her fans would be in one of those categories, especially since Swift's appeal has tended to be with her generation and with older fans. According to Statista.com, Spotify, on the other hand, is focused on its "user-curated play-list, which can be shared publicly or between friends," which is heavily used by users aged 20 and under.[25] Logically, then, by pulling her music from Spotify, Swift was not necessarily risking making her music unavailable from her long-time fans. Yet, at the same time, she could call attention to artists' rights, the differences in royalty rates among various streaming services, and between streaming services and sales of digital music.

Even after her highly publicized standoffs with Apple Music and Spotify, Swift continues to serve as an outspoken advocate for songwriters and performing musicians. Swift's contributions to music and the seriousness with which she takes music and the recognition of songwriters were recognized by the performing rights licensing agency BMI, which established the Taylor Swift Award in 2016.[26] Swift was the first winner of the award.

It seems that in the case of many singer-songwriters, there is one particular trait for which they are best known. With Taylor Swift, it is the fact that she focuses extensively on her personal life in her compositions. Although some of her fans may have dealt with similar experiences and had to work their way through similar emotional journeys, Swift has made it clear that her songs are about her experiences and feelings. She may offer songs as warnings to others—as she had done, based on the "hidden" messages in the printed lyrics on her first several albums—but virtually all of her major works are based on personal experience. Unfortunately for Swift, she seems to have had more than her fair share of losses in love. Perhaps just as unfortunate from an artistic perspective, Swift's tendency to dwell on her personal life has left both her and her work vulnerable to parody. For example, in October 2015, after tabloid reports—which proved not to be true—that Swift had broken up with then boyfriend Calvin Harris after he was photographed allegedly emerging from a Los Angeles massage parlor of ill repute, comedian Steve DiMatteo wrote a spoof article for the *Huffington Post* that purported to list track titles for her upcoming, post-Harris album. The basis of the humor was that Swift's highly publicized breakups tend to lead to more than enough new material to form the basis of the singer-songwriter's next real-life album. Included in DiMatteo's parody were titles such as "I'll Stop Writing about Breakups When You Stop Buying My Albums" as well as others that referenced Harris's alleged activities at the massage parlor. Part of DiMatteo's parody also revolved around Swift's extensive use of social media: one alleged track was "You Won't Believe How Many Pinterest Boards I'm Making about You Right Now."[27] Despite the fact that the alleged October 2015 breakup was not true, when rumors began circulating in late May and early June 2016 that the couple had indeed broken up for real, the media widely reported that the breakup was causing fans to anticipate a new album.[28] To put it another way, Taylor Swift's fans continued to associate her work almost solely with her personal trials and tribulations in love. Interestingly, Taylor Swift is not the first singer-songwriter to focus extensively on her or his own personal difficulties. Ironically, perhaps one of the best-known confessional singer-songwriters of the past, James Taylor in the early part of his career—when the singer-songwriter movement of the early 1970s was just starting—is the musician for whom Taylor Swift was named.

Notes

CHAPTER 1

1. Elias Leight, "Taylor Swift's Samizdat Songwriting: An Expert Weighs In," *Billboard* 128 (December 17, 2016), p. 44.
2. Chris Willman, quoted in Brian Mansfield, "*Red* Puts Swift in Rarefied Company," *USA Today* (October 31, 2012), Life section, 3d.
3. One of the most interesting exchanges of widely diverging views of the feministic nature of Swift's work can be seen in Rachel McCarthy James, "Swift Judgment," *Bitch Magazine: Feminist Response to Pop Culture* 50 (Spring 2011), pp. 15–21, and Lora Zorian, Letter to the Editor, *Bitch Magazine: Feminist Response to Popular Culture* 51 (Summer 2011), p. 4, the latter of which was written in response to Rachel McCarthy James's article.
4. Richard Washington, " 'Swifties' Take a Gamble on Taylor's Love in Chinese Online Marketplace," *CNBC.com* (June 27, 2016), http://www.cnbc.com/2016/06/27/swifties-take-a-gamble-on-taylors-love-in-chinese-online-marketplace.html, accessed June 28, 2016.
5. The Editors of *Rolling Stone*, "Mellow Gold," *Rolling Stone* 1180 (April 11, 2013), p. 57.
6. Lester Bangs, "James Taylor Marked for Death," *Who Put the Bomp* 8 (Fall–Winter 1971), 59+. Reprinted in Lester Bangs, *Psychotic Reactions and Carburetor Dung* (New York, NY: Vintage Books, 1988), pp. 53–81.

CHAPTER 2

1. The Editors of *BMI News*, "Songwriter Taylor Swift Signs Publishing Deal with Sony/ATV," *BMI News* (May 12, 2005), www.bmi.com/news/

entry/20050512Taylor_Swift_Songwriter_Taylor_Swift_Signs_Publishing_Deal _With_, accessed February 24, 2016.

2. See, Ed Christman, "The Top 10 Stories of the Year: 4. Taylor Swift Sells 1 Million Albums," *Billboard* 122 (December 18, 2010), p. 24, in which it is noted that approximately 75 percent of the one million copies of *Speak Now* that were sold in the album's first week were physical CDs; and Ed Christman, Keith Caulfield, and William Gruger, "The Taylor Swift Playbook in 6 (Not So Easy) Steps," *Billboard* 126 (November 15, 2014), pp. 13–14, which focuses on the high number of physical CD sales of *1989*.

3. Stevie Nicks, "The 2010 *Time* 100: Taylor Swift," *Time.com* (April 29, 2010), content.time.com/time/specials/packages/article/0,28804,1984685_1984940 _1985536,00.html, accessed February 29, 2016.

4. "Download This!" *People* 66 (November 8, 2006), pp. 27–30.

5. Brian Mansfield, "On the Verge," *USA Today* (November 21, 2006), Life section, 5d.

6. Ralph Novak, "Taylor Swift," *People* 66 (November 20, 2006), p. 49.

7. Jeff Tamarkin, "*Taylor Swift*," All Music Guide, www.allmusic.com/album/ release/taylor-swift-mr0001279067, accessed March 10, 2016.

8. The Editors of Allmusic.com, "*Taylor Swift*: Awards," www.allmusic.com/ album/taylor-swift-mw0000550301/awards, accessed March 8, 2016.

9. The analysis of *Fearless* is based largely on James E. Perone, "Taylor Swift: *Fearless*," in James E. Perone, ed., *The Album: A Guide to Pop Music's Most Provocative, Influential, and Important Creations*, vol. 4 (Santa Barbara, CA: Praeger Publishers, 2012), pp. 185–189.

10. Incidentally, West's infamous interruption of Swift's speech prompted U.S. president Barack Obama to call the rapper an "asshole" and prompted celebrity Katie Perry to tweet "Fuck U Kanye." For details, see Tim Stack, "Kanye Steals the Spotlight," *Entertainment Weekly* 1067 (September 25, 2009), pp. 11–13. As discussed later, the battle between Swift and West has continued well into 2016.

11. Taylor Swift, liner notes for *Fearless*, CD, Big Machine Records BMRATS0200, 2008.

12. The Editors of *Rolling Stone*, "Buy These Now," *Rolling Stone* 1066 (November 27, 2008), p. 121.

13. Elysa Gardner, "Taylor Swift Hits All the Right Words," *USA Today* (November 11, 2008), p. 5d.

14. Members of Def Leppard, in *CMT Crossroads: Taylor Swift & Def Leppard*, DVD, Big Machine Records BMRATD 0100, 2009.

15. See, for example, Louis Hau, Ed Christman, and Craig Marks, "The Only Girl in the World," *Billboard* 122 (November 13, 2010), p. 5; and Tom Roland, "Princess Superstar," *Billboard* 122 (October 23, 2010), pp. 18–21, both of which include discussion of Swift's intergenerational popularity.

CHAPTER 3

1. Taylor Swift, Liner notes to *Speak Now*, CD, Big Machine Records BMRTS0350A, 2010, p. 1.

2. Ibid., p. 2.

3. Jon Dolan, "Taylor Crashes a Wedding," *Rolling Stone* 1116 (October 28, 2010), p. 62.

4. Taylor Swift, Liner notes to *1989*, CD, Big Machine Records BMRBD0550A, 2014.

5. Madeline Boardman, "John Mayer: 'I'm Not a Womanizer, but I Am a Recovered Ego Addict,'" *US Magazine* online (March 6, 2015), www.usmagazine .com/celebrity-news/news/john-mayer-im-not-a-womanizer-but-i-am-a-recovered -ego-addict-201563, accessed March 21, 2016.

6. Julie Miller, "Photos: Five Reasons to Think Taylor Swift Is John Mayer's 'Paper Doll,'" *Vanity Fair* (June 19, 2013), www.vanityfair.com/hollywood/2013/ 06/taylor-swift-paper-doll-photos, accessed March 21, 2016.

7. The battle-in-song was even covered by more prestigious publications. See, for example, Jon Caramanica, "Taylor Swift Is Angry, Darn It," *New York Times* 160 (October 24, 2010), www.nytimes.com/2010/10/24/arts/music/ 24swift.html?_r=0, accessed February 9, 2016.

8. Elio Iannacci, " 'Everyone I Know Has Had Fair Warning!' " *Maclean's* 123 (November 8, 2010), p. 117.

9. The Editors of *Rolling Stone*, "100 Greatest Country Songs of All Time," *Rolling Stone* 1211 (June 1, 2014), www.rollingstone.com/music/pictures/100-greatest -country-songs-of-all-time-20140601/24-taylor-swift-mean-2010-0238068, accessed February 26, 2016.

10. The Editors of *Rolling Stone*, "100 Greatest Country Songs of All Time," *Rolling Stone* (June 1, 2014), www.rollingstone.com/music/pictures/100-greatest -country-songs-of-all-time-20140601/24-taylor-swift-mean-2010-0238068, accessed January 29, 2016.

11. The Editors of All Music Guide, "*Speak Now*: Awards," www.allmusic.com/ album/speak-now-mw0002025410/awards, accessed April 8, 2016.

12. James Christopher Monger, "*World Tour Live: Speak Out*," All Music Guide, http://www.allmusic.com/album/world-tour-live-speak-now-mw0002232035, accessed July 5, 2016.

13. Jon Dolan, "Taylor's Great Pop Adventure," *Rolling Stone* 1169 (November 8, 2012), p. 66.

14. Taylor Swift, Liner notes for *Red*, CD, Big Machine Records BMR310400A, 2012, p. 1.

15. The banjitar, or ganjo, is a six-stringed banjo tuned like a guitar.

16. Patrick Doyle, "Swift's Bold New Direction," *Rolling Stone* 1165 (September 13, 2012), pp. 17–18.

17. The Editors of All Music Guide, "*Red*: Awards," www.allmusic.com/album/ red-mw0002414735/awards, accessed April 19, 2016.

18. Heather Phares, "*The Hunger Games: Songs from District 12 and Beyond*," All Music Guide, www.allmusic.com/album/the-hunger-games-songs-from -district-12-and-beyond-mw0002308080, accessed May 23, 2016.

CHAPTER 4

1. Taylor Swift, "*One Chance* Music Video: 'Sweeter than Fiction' by Taylor Swift," www.youtube.com/watch?v=rO321-9MHYc, accessed May 12, 2016.

2. Jem Aswad, "Taylor Swift, *1989*," *Billboard* 126 (November 1, 2014), pp. 69–70.

3. Stephen Thomas Erlewine, "*1989*: Review," All Music Guide, www.allmusic.com/album/1989-mw0002726289, accessed April 22, 2016.

4. Taylor Swift, Liner notes to *1989*, CD, Big Machine Records BMRBD0550A, 2014.

5. Daniel D'Addario, "Taylor Swift's 'Welcome to New York' Is a New Kind of Equality Anthem," *Time.com* (October 21, 2014), time.com/3528687/taylor-swift-welcome-to-new-york-1989-new-track-gay/, accessed February 17, 2016.

6. Nolan Feeney, "Taylor Swift's 'Welcome to New York' Is the Musical Equivalent of a Peppermint Latte," *Time.com* (October 20, 2014), time.com/3525590/taylor-swift-welcome-to-new-york-full/, accessed February 17, 2016.

7. Daniel D'Addario, "Taylor Swift Silences 'Welcome to New York' Critics, Donates to Public Schools," *Time.com* (October 29, 2014), time.com/3546081/taylor-swift-welcome-to-new-york-public-schools/, accessed February 17, 2016.

8. The "Shake It Off" outtake video is available as a link at the end of the following online article: Erin Strecker, "Taylor Swift Shocks Fans in New 'Shake It Off' Outtakes Video," *Billboard* (October 9, 2014), www.billboard.com/articles/6281279/taylor-swift-shake-it-off-outtakes-video, accessed May 3, 2016.

9. Taylor Swift, " 'I Know Places,' " *1989* "D.L.X." edition, CD, Big Machine Records BMRBD0550A, 2014.

10. Taylor Swift, " 'I Wish You Would,' " *1989* "D.L.X." edition, CD, Big Machine Records BMRBD0550A, 2014.

11. Taylor Swift, " 'Blank Space,' " *1989* "D.L.X." edition, CD, Big Machine Records BMRBD0550A, 2014.

12. Jem Aswad, "Taylor Swift, *1989*," *Billboard* 126 (November 1, 2014), pp. 69–70.

13. Keith Caulfield, "Happy B-Day, *1989*! Taylor Swift Spends Full Year at the Top," *Billboard* 127 (November 7, 2015), pp. 60–61.

CHAPTER 5

1. Erin Strecker, "Remember When Taylor Swift Shined As *Saturday Night Live* Host?" *Billboard* (January 2, 2015), http://www.billboard.com/articles/columns/pop-shop/6429325/taylor-swift-saturday-night-live-host-flashback, accessed June 8, 2016.

2. Heather Phares, "*Hannah Montana: The Movie*," All Music Guide, www.allmusic.com/album/hannah-montana-the-movie-mw0000804688, accessed May 23, 2016.

3. Nolan Feeney, " 'Wildest Dreams' Director Defends Taylor Swift Video Against Whitewashing," *Time.com* (September 2, 2015), time.com/4020783/taylor-swift-wildest-dreams-director-defends-controversy/, accessed February 17, 2016.

CHAPTER 6

1. Trevor Anderson, "Swift Approval: Taylor Swift's Favorite Covers of Her Songs," *Billboard* (September 17, 2015), www.billboard.com/articles/columns/pop-shop/6443857/taylor-swift-favorite-covers-of-her-songs, accessed May 23, 2016.

2. Ibid.

3. The transcript of the telephone conversation between Swift and West that came to light suggests that there may have been less conflict between the two artists than what was portrayed in the media. See Raisa Bruner, "Read the Transcript of Kanye West's Phone Call with Taylor Swift," *Time.com* (July 19, 2016), http://time.com/4410370/taylor-swift-kim-kardashian-kanye-west/, accessed February 1, 2017.
4. Elias Leight, "Taylor Swift's Samizdat Songwriting: An Expert Weighs In," *Billboard* 128 (December 17, 2016), p. 44.
5. Ibid.

CHAPTER 7

1. Yahoo music writer Chris Willman, quoted in Brian Mansfield, "*Red* Puts Swift in Rarefied Company," *USA Today* (October 31, 2012), Life section, p. 3d.
2. Katie Hasty, "Swift's Un-Swift Climb," *Billboard* 119 (August 4, 2007), p. 9.
3. Tom Roland, "Princess Superstar," *Billboard* 122 (October 23, 2010), pp. 18–21.
4. Louis Hau, Ed Christman, and Craig Marks, "The Only Girl in the World," *Billboard* 122 (November 13, 2010), p. 5.
5. See George Stark, "Taylor Swift and Nicki Minaj Clash on Twitter over MTV VMA Nominations," *Time.com* (July 22, 2015), time.com/3967305/taylor -swift-nicki-minaj-twitter/, accessed February 17, 2016, as an example of media coverage of this brief social media spat between Swift and Minaj.
6. As an example of how Swift, Kardashian, and West have publicly sparred using social media, as well as the media's coverage of the conflict, see the Editors of CNN, "Bad Blood: Kim, Kanye and Taylor Clash on Social Media," *CNN.com* (July 18, 2016), http://www.cnn.com/videos/entertainment/2016/07/18/ tds-taylor-swift-kardashian-feud.cnn, accessed July 19, 2016.
7. Shaun Cullen, "The Innocent and the Runaway: Kanye West, Taylor Swift, and the Cultural Politics of Racial Melodrama," *Journal of Popular Music Studies* 28 (March 2016), pp. 33–50.
8. Emily White, "Swift, Harris Team for Social Gain," *Billboard* 128 (April 2, 2016), p. 71.
9. Sophie Vokes-Dudgeon, "Taylor Swift Grants Terminally Ill 4-Year-Old's Final Wish, Talks via FaceTime with Cancer Patient," *US Magazine* (March 4, 2015), www.usmagazine.com/celebrity-news/news/taylor-swift-grants-terminally-ill- 4-year-olds-final-wish——watch-201543, accessed February 18, 2016.
10. Sasha Geffen, "Taylor Swift Snapped Selfies and Shared Smiles with Fans Battling Cancer," *MTV News* (July 12, 2016), http://www.mtv.com/news/2903825/ taylor-swift-childrens-hospital-australia/, accessed July 12, 2016.
11. David Beer, "Making Friends with Jarvis Cocker: Music Culture in the Context of Web 2.0," *Cultural Sociology* 2 (2008), p. 233.
12. Nancy K. Baym, "Fans or Friends?: Seeing Social Media Audiences as Musicians Do," *Participations: Journal of Audience & Reception Studies* 9 (November 2012), p. 287.
13. Melissa Click, Hyunji Lee, and Holly Willson Holladay, "Making Monsters: Lady Gaga, Fan Identification, and Social Media," *Popular Music and Society* 36 (no. 3, 2013), pp. 360–379.

14. See, for example, Jefferson Graham, "App Makes It a Cinch to Add Backup Band," *USA Today* (January 21, 2016), Money section, p. 3b.

15. See Jayme Deerwester, "How Was Your Day?" *USA Today* (February 17, 2016), Life section, p. 1d, for press coverage of Swift's comments to female artists.

16. Associated Press, "Taylor Swift Donating $1 Million to Louisiana," *CNBC.com*, http://www.cnbc.com/2016/08/17/taylor-swift-donating-1-million-to-louisiana.html, accessed August 17, 2016.

17. See Rachel McCarthy James, "Swift Judgment," *Bitch Magazine: Feminist Response to Pop Culture* 50 (Spring 2011), pp. 15–21, and Lora Zorian, Letter to the Editor, *Bitch Magazine: Feminist Response to Popular Culture* 51 (Summer 2011), p. 4.

18. Janet Albrechtsen, "The Corruption of Feminism," *Policy* 31 (Winter 2015), pp. 3–6.

19. Taylor Vidmar, "Dear Gloria Steinem: Let Me Make My Own Decisions, Please," *MTV News* (February 9, 2016), http://www.mtv.com/news/2737554/dear-gloria-steinem-let-me-make-my-own-decisions-please/?xrs=_s.tw_news, accessed July 18, 2016.

20. Tim Bajarin, "How Taylor Swift Saved Apple Music," *Time* (June 30, 2015), time.com/3940500/apple-music-taylor-swift-release/, accessed February 17, 2016.

21. See, for example, Sarah Caspari, "Apple's Tweet to Taylor Swift: 'We Hear You,' " *Christian Science Monitor* (June 22, 2015), www.csmonitor.com/Business/2015/0622/Apple-s-tweet-to-Taylor-Swift-We-hear-you-video, accessed February 8, 2016.

22. Alan Light, "Taylor Swift," *Billboard* 126 (December 13, 2014), pp. 64–71.

23. Victor Luckerson, "Why Only Taylor Swift Could Leave Spotify," *Time* (November 5, 2014), time.com/3556721/taylor-swift-spotify-1989/, accessed February 17, 2016.

24. The Editors of Statista.com, "Number of Pandora's Active Users from 2009 to 2015 (in Millions)," (n.d.), www.statista.com/statistics/190989/active-users-of-music-streaming-service-pandora-since-2009/, accessed May 20, 2016.

25. The Editors of Statista.com, "Number of Global Monthly Active Spotify Users from July 2012 to January 2016 (in Millions)," (n.d.), www.statista.com/statistics/367739/spotify-global-mau/, accessed May 20, 2016.

26. Molly Driscoll, "What Is the Taylor Swift Award? Singer Receives Prize at 2016 BMI Pop Awards," *Christian Science Monitor* (May 11, 2016), www.csmonitor.com/The-Culture/Music/2016/0511/What-is-the-Taylor-Swift-Award-Singer-receives-prize-at-2016-BMI-Pop-Awards, accessed June 2, 2016.

27. Steve DiMatteo, "Track List for Taylor Swift's New Album Leaked," *Huffington Post* (October 13, 2015), www.huffingtonpost.com/steve-dimatteo/track-list-for-taylor-swi_b_8281980.html, accessed June 3, 2016.

28. See, for example, Sierra Marquina, "Taylor Swift, Calvin Harris Split: 'Love Is Dead' and More of the Best Internet Reactions," *US Magazine* (June 1, 2016), www.usmagazine.com/celebrity-news/news/taylor-swift-calvin-harris-split-best-internet-reactions-w208539, accessed June 3, 2016.

Annotated Discography

Taylor Swift. Taylor Swift, acoustic guitar and vocals; Bruce Bouton, Dobro; Mike Brignardello, bass; Nick Buda, drums; Gary Burnette, electric guitar; Nathan Chapman, guitars, banjo, bass, drums, backing vocals, mandolin, piano; Eric Darken, percussion; Dan Dugmore, pedal steel guitar; Shannon Forrest, drums; Rob Hajacos, fiddle; Tony Harrell, keyboards; Jeff Hyde, banjo; Andy Leftwich, fiddle and mandolin; Liana Manis, backing vocals; Tim Marks, bass; Robert Ellis Orrall, backing vocals; Lex Price, mandolin; Scotty Sanders, Dobro and pedal steel guitar; Ilya Toshinsky,[1] banjo and acoustic guitar; Wanda Vick, fiddle; John Willis, banjo, acoustic guitar, mandolin. "Tim McGraw" (Taylor Swift, Liz Rose), "Picture to Burn" (Swift, Rose), "Teardrops on My Guitar (Swift, Rose), "A Place in This World" (Swift, Robert Ellis Orrall, Angelo Petraglia), "Cold as You" (Swift, Rose), "The Outside" (Swift), "Tied Together with a Smile" (Swift, Rose), "Stay Beautiful" (Swift, Rose), "Should've Said No" (Swift), "Mary's Song (Oh My My My)" (Swift, Rose, Brian Maher), "Our Song" (Swift). Executive producer, Scott Borchetta. Produced by Nathan Chapman. String arrangements by Nathan Yudkin. CD, Big Machine Records BMR079102, 2006. The various subsequent editions of the album that were released in 2006–2008 included bonus tracks and music videos. Among the songs available on subsequent editions that were not included on the original release were "I'm Only Me When I'm with You" (Swift, Orrall, Petraglia), "Invisible" (Swift, Orrall), and "Perfectly Good Heart" (Swift, Brett James, Troy Verges). Swift's self-titled debut album reached the Top 10 on the country album charts at the time of its initial release. It has reappeared on the country charts in subsequent years. Even before the release of the album,

---

[1]The artist's name is sometimes given as Ilya Toshinsky and sometimes as Ilya Toshinkiy. I have included the spelling variations as they are presented in the liner notes in Swift's CD booklets.

"Tim McGraw" became one of Swift's signature songs. Several singles that were released from the album were genuine hits, including "Teardrops on My Guitar," "Picture to Burn," "Our Song," and "Should've Said No."

Fearless. Taylor Swift, acoustic guitar and vocals; Andrew Bowers, finger snaps; Nicholas Brown, finger snaps; Nick Buda, drums; Colbie Caillat, backing vocals; Nathan Chapman, guitars, keyboards, mandolin, percussion, piano, and backing vocals; Carolyn Cooper, finger snaps; Burrus Cox, finger snaps; Eric Darken, percussion, vibraphone; Lauren Elcan, finger snaps; Caitlin Evanson, backing vocals; Kenny Greenberg, electric guitar; Rob Hajacos, fiddle; Tony Harrell, piano, organ, keyboards; Amos Heller, bass; Claire Indie, cello; John Keefe, drums; Tim Lauer, keyboards, piano, organ; Tim Marks, bass; Delaney McBride, finger snaps; Emma McBride, finger snaps; Grant Mikelson, electric guitar; Bryan Sutton, acoustic guitar and mandolin; Ilya Toshinsky, banjo; Alan Wilson, percussion. "Fearless" (Taylor Swift, Liz Rose, Hillary Lindsey), "Fifteen" (Swift), "Love Story" (Swift), "Hey Stephen" (Swift), "White Horse" (Swift, Rose), "You Belong with Me" (Swift), "Breathe" (Swift, Colbie Caillat), "Tell Me Why" (Swift, Rose), "You're Not Sorry" (Swift), "The Way I Loved You" (Swift, John Rich), "Forever & Always" (Swift), "The Best Day" (Swift), "Change" (Swift). Executive producer, Scott Borchetta. Produced by Nathan Chapman and Taylor Swift. CD, Big Machine Records BMRATS0200, 2008. Although Swift's debut album and its singles were commercially successful, *Fearless* established Swift as a well-rounded and well-known star. *Fearless* topped the *Billboard* 200, the Country Albums, the Top Internet Albums, and various other charts. "Love Story," "White Horse," "You Belong with Me," and "Fearless" all performed well on the singles charts. At the 2009 Grammy Awards, *Fearless* was named Album of the Year and Best Country Album. Liz Rose and Swift won the Grammy for Best Country Song for "White Horse." Swift won an additional Grammy for Best Female Country Vocal Performance for "White Horse."

Speak Now. Taylor Swift, acoustic guitar, vocals, hand claps; Nick Buda, drums; Nathan Chapman, guitars, banjo, mandolin, bass, percussion, organ, piano, keyboards, backing vocals; Smith Curry, lap steel guitar; Caitlin Evanson, harmony vocals; Shannon Forrest, drums; John Gardner, drums; Rob Hajacos, fiddle; Amos Heller, bass; Liz Huett, backing vocals; Tim Lauer, organ and piano; Tim Marks, bass; Mike Meadows, electric guitar and hand claps; Grant Mickelson, electric guitar; Paul Sidoti, electric guitar; Tommy Sims, bass; Bryan Sutton, acoustic guitar; Al Wilson, percussion and hand claps. "Mine" (Taylor Swift), "Sparks Fly" (Swift), "Back to December" (Swift), "Speak Now" (Swift), "Dear John" (Swift), "Mean" (Swift), "The Story of Us" (Swift), "Never Grow Up" (Swift), "Enchanted" (Swift), "Better than Revenge" (Swift), "Innocent" (Swift), "Haunted" (Swift), "Last Kiss" (Swift), "Long Live" (Swift). Executive producer, Scott Borchetta. Produced by Nathan Chapman and Taylor Swift. String arrangements by Paul Buckmaster and Chris Carmichael. CD, Big Machine Records BMRTS0350A, 2010. Like its predecessor, *Speak Now* topped the *Billboard* 200 and Country Album charts as well as several other record charts. The album also spawned several hit singles, including "Sparks Fly," "Back to December," "Mean," and "Mine." Although *Speak Now* did not win any Grammys, Swift won Grammys for Best Country Song and Best Country Solo Performance for "Mean."

Red. Taylor Swift, acoustic guitar and vocals; Peggy Baldwin, cello; Brett Banducci, viola; Jeff Bhasker, bass, piano, keyboards, backing vocals; J. Bonilla, drums, percussion; Nick Buda, drums; Tom Bukovac, electric guitar; Nathan Chapman, guitars, keyboards, mandolin, piano, bass, backing vocals; Daphne Chen, violin; Lauren Chipman, viola; Eric Darken, percussion; Marcia Dickstein, harp; Richard Dodd, cello; Caitlin Evanson, backing vocals; Paul Franklin, steel guitar; Eric Gorfain, violin; Dann Huff, electric guitar, bouzouki, "high string" guitar; Tyler Johnson, backing vocals; Charlie Judge, accordion, organ, piano, string synthesizer; Gina Kronstadt, violin; John Krovoza, cello; Marisa Kuney, violin; Jacknife Lee, bass, guitar, keyboards; Gary Lightbody, backing vocals; Max Martin, keyboards; Anders Mouridsen, guitar; Jamie Muhoberac, piano; Nell Nikolaeva, violin; Radu Pieptea, violin; Simeon Pillich, contrabass; Wes Precourt, violin; Bill Rieflin, drums; Ed Sheeran, vocals; Shellback, bass, guitars, keyboards; Jake Sinclair, backing vocals; Jimmie Sloas, bass; Aaron Sterling, drums; Jeff Takiguchi, contrabass; Andy Thompson, guitar, electric piano; Ilya Toshinskiy, mandolin; Butch Walker, drums, percussion, backing vocals; Amy Wickman, violin; Dan Wilson, guitar, bass, piano, backing vocals; Rodney Wirtz, viola; Jonathan Yudkin, fiddle. "State of Grace" (Taylor Swift), "Red" (Swift), "Treacherous" (Swift, Dan Wilson), "I Knew You Were Trouble" (Swift, Max Martin, Shellback), "All Too Well" (Swift, Liz Rose), "22" (Swift, Martin, Shellback), "I Almost Do" (Swift), "We Are Never Ever Getting Back Together" (Swift, Martin, Shellback), "Stay Stay Stay" (Swift), "The Last Time" (Swift, Gary Lightbody, Jacknife Lee), "Holy Ground" (Swift), "Sad Beautiful Tragic" (Swift), "The Lucky One" (Swift), "Everything Has Changed" (Swift, Ed Sheeran), "Starlight" (Swift), "Begin Again" (Swift). Executive producer, Scott Borchetta. Various track producers. CD, Big Machine Records BMR310400A, 2012. Like its two predecessors, *Red* topped the *Billboard* 200 and the country album charts as well as various other record charts. The album produced several hit singles, including "We Are Never Ever Getting Back Together," "State of Grace," "Red," "Begin Again," and "I Knew You Were Trouble."

1989. Taylor Swift, acoustic guitar, handclaps, and vocals; Jack Antonoff, bass, drums, guitars, keyboards, backing vocals; Nathan Chapman, guitars, bass, drums, keyboards; Imogen Heap, drums, percussion, keyboards, backing vocals; Greg Kurstin, keyboards; Jonas Lindeborg, trumpet; Max Martin, piano, keyboards, handclaps, backing vocals; Mattman & Robin, bass, guitar, drums, keyboards, percussion; Ali Payami, keyboards; Shellback, guitars, bass, drums, percussion, percussive effects, backing vocals; Ryan Tedder, guitars, piano, keyboards, backing vocals; Jonas Thander, saxophone; Magnus Wiklund, trombone; Noel Zancanella, bass, synthesizer. "Welcome to New York" (Taylor Swift, Ryan Tedder), "Blank Space" (Swift, Max Martin, Shellback), "Style" (Swift, Martin, Shellback, Ali Payami), "Out of the Woods" (Swift, Jack Antonoff), "All You Had to Do Was Stay" (Swift, Martin), "Shake It Off" (Swift, Martin, Shellback), "I Wish You Would" (Swift, Antonoff), "Bad Blood" (Swift, Martin, Shellback), "Wildest Dreams" (Swift, Martin, Shellback), "How You Get the Girl" (Swift, Martin, Shellback), "This Love" (Swift), "I Know Places" (Swift, Tedder), "Clean" (Swift, Imogen Heap). Executive producers, Max Martin and Taylor Swift. Various track producers. String arrangements by Mattias Bylund. CD, Big Machine Records BMRBD0550A, 2014. Because of the pop nature of

1989, it did not appear on the country charts. It did, however, top the *Billboard* 200 and various Internet, streaming, and download charts. "Out of the Woods," "Shake It Off," "Wildest Dreams," "Style," "Bad Blood," and "Blank Space" were all significant hit singles from the album. In 2016, *1989* won the Grammy Awards for Best Pop Vocal Album and Album of the Year. In addition, Swift won the Grammy for Best Music Video for "Bad Blood."

Annotated Bibliography

Albrechtsen, Janet. "The Corruption of Feminism." *Policy* 31 (Winter 2015), 3–6. The author claims that public figures such as Swift and actress Gwyneth Paltrow are widely viewed as feminists, but that they actually represent a corrupted form of feminism.

Alter, Charlotte. "Taylor Swift Just Removed Her Music from Spotify: And Spotify Can't Shake It Off." *Time* (November 3, 2014), time.com/3554438/taylor-swift-spotify/. Accessed May 19, 2016. A brief report on Swift's battle with the Spotify streaming audio service over artists' royalties.

Anderson, Kyle. "Breaking Down 'Bad Blood' by the Numbers." *Entertainment Weekly* 1365/1366 (May 29, 2015), 20. A report on the music video for "Bad Blood."

Anderson, Trevor. "Swift Approval: Taylor Swift's Favorite Covers of Her Songs." *Billboard* (September 17, 2015), www.billboard.com/articles/columns/pop-shop/6443857/taylor-swift-favorite-covers-of-her-songs. Accessed May 23, 2016. A listing and brief description of Swift's favorite covers of her songs. Interestingly, several versions of "Shake It Off" are included.

Arnold, Chuck. "*Speak Now*." *People* 74 (November 8, 2010), 43. A somewhat mixed review of the album, which criticizes Swift's vocal technique and the "heavy production" on "Haunted" and some other songs.

Aswad, Jem. "The NSA's Got Nothing Compared with Taylor Swift." *Billboard* 126 (November 8, 2014), 14. A report on security measures that Swift and Big Machine Records put into place to ensure that none of the songs on *1989* would be leaked.

Aswad, Jem. "Taylor Swift, *1989*." *Billboard* 126 (November 1, 2014), 69–70. A largely favorable review that focuses on Swift's stylistic changes and increased lyrical sophistication.

Aswad, Jem. "Taylor Swift and Country: Splitsville!" *Billboard* 126 (August 30, 2014), 13–14. A report on Swift's 2012 album *Red* and the 2014 single "Shake It Off" and how they represent a move from country to pop.

Ayers, Mike. "Grammys 2016: The Winners List." *Wall Street Journal* Online Edition (February 16, 2016), blogs.wsj.com/speakeasy/2016/02/15/grammys-2016 -winners-list/. Accessed March 3, 2016.

Bajarin, Tim. "How Taylor Swift Saved Apple Music." *Time* (June 30, 2015), time.com/3940500/apple-music-taylor-swift-release/. Accessed February 17, 2016. According to Bajarin, Swift's campaign caused Apple Music to do what was completely unexpected: "change its mind."

Bartolomeo, Joey. "Inside Taylor's World." *People* 74 (November 1, 2010), 52–57. A feature-length profile of Swift.

Baym, Nancy K. "Fans or Friends?: Seeing Social Media Audiences as Musicians Do." *Participations: Journal of Audience & Reception Studies* 9 (November 2012), 286–316. Although this scholarly study does not deal specifically with Taylor Swift, many of the author's findings seem to pertain to Swift's use of social media as a means of bonding with her fans.

Beer, David. "Making Friends with Jarvis Cocker: Music Culture in the Context of Web 2.0." *Cultural Sociology* 2 (2008), 222–241. This article analyzes the use of social media by musicians and the changes that this use has caused in the relationship between musicians and their audiences.

Bethell, Laura. "Taylor Swift." *Maverick* 81 (April 2009), 48–53. A profile of Swift.

Biedenharn, Isabella. "Taylor Swift Schools Us Again." *Entertainment Weekly* 1374 (July 31, 2015), 14. A brief article on Swift's responses to grammatical errors that she spotted on the Internet, in song lyrics, and so on.

Bohannon, John. "From James Taylor to Taylor Swift: Music Evolves like Biological Organisms." *Science Now* (May 5, 2015), 1. The author describes research into the evolution of music that ties it to biological evolution.

Browne, David. "Ryan Adams' Most Unlikely Hit Ever." *Rolling Stone* 1246 (October 22, 2015), 14. A report on Adams's album *1989*, which features acoustic covers of Swift's *1989*.

Browne, David. "Ukuleles Rock: Little Axes Earn Big Fans." *Rolling Stone* 1133 (June 23, 2011), 32. This article on the newfound popularity of the ukulele opens with a quote from Swift about how well she believes the instrument fits her live performances of "Fearless."

Bruner, Raisa. "Read the Transcript of Kanye West's Phone Call with Taylor Swift." *Time.com* (July 19, 2016), http://time.com/4410370/taylor-swift-kim -kardashian-kanye-west/. Accessed February 1, 2017. Interestingly, this transcript of the highly publicized "feud" between Swift, Kanye West, and Kim Kardashian suggests that the professional relationship between Swift and West is closer than what the media portrays.

Bruno, Antony. "The Top 10 Stories of the Year: 9. Music Apps Go Mainstream." *Billboard* 122 (December 18, 2010), 24. A brief report that includes mention of Swift's smartphone app that encourages downloads of Swift's songs by her fans and that allows fans to remix tracks and add their own vocals.

Bullivant, Stephen. "A Theology of Taylor Swift." *America* 214 (June 6, 2016), 33–34. The theological basis and threads that connect Swift's "Our Song," "Christmas Must Be Something More," "Fifteen," and "Never Grow Up" are discussed as well as Swift's relationship with other pop singer-songwriters who use religious references in their material.

Butler, Susan. "Growing Pains." *Billboard* 117 (May 21, 2005), 14. A brief profile of the early promise shown by "15-year-old songwriter/artist Taylor Swift."

Caramanica, Jon. "My Music, MySpace, My Life." *New York Times* 158 (November 9, 2008), www.nytimes.com/2008/11/09/arts/music/09cara.html. Accessed February 2, 2016. An article on Swift's control of her image through the use of social media and her control of fans' photographs of her.

Caramanica, Jon. "No More Kid Stuff for Taylor Swift." *New York Times* 162 (October 28, 2012), www.nytimes.com/2012/10/28/arts/music/no-more-kid-stuff-for-taylor-swift.html?_r=0. Accessed February 15, 2016. According to this favorable review of *Red*, Swift's main growth on the album is "musical rather than experiential."

Caramanica, Jon. "The Purpler the Bruise, the Sweeter the Song." *New York Times* 160 (December 19, 2010), www.nytimes.com/2010/12/19/arts/music/19caramanica.html?_r=0. Accessed February 9, 2016. A brief review of *Speak Now* in which the author notes increased bite in Swift's lyrics.

Caramanica, Jon. "Taylor Swift Is Angry, Darn It." *New York Times* 160 (October 24, 2010), www.nytimes.com/2010/10/24/arts/music/24swift.html?_r=0. Accessed February 9, 2016. A report on Swift's putdown of ex-boyfriend John Mayer on "Dear John," a song that includes elements of Mayer's musical style.

Caramanica, Jon. "A Young Outsider's Life Turned Inside Out." *New York Times* 157 (September 7, 2008), www.nytimes.com/2008/09/07/arts/music/07cara.html. Accessed February 2, 2016. A report on Swift's inspiration for the material on her debut album: being an outsider in school.

Caspari, Sarah. "Apple's Tweet to Taylor Swift: 'We Hear You.'" *Christian Science Monitor* (June 22, 2015), www.csmonitor.com/Business/2015/0622/Apple-s-tweet-to-Taylor-Swift-We-hear-you-video. Accessed February 8, 2016. A report on Swift's Tumblr post going viral and apparently causing Apple to rethink its refusal to pay royalties to artists whose music was streamed during Apple Music's free trial period.

Caulfield, Keith. "Happy B-Day, *1989*! Taylor Swift Spends Full Year at the Top." *Billboard* 127 (November 7, 2015), 60–61. A report on *1989* spending an entire year in the *Billboard* 200. The author compares *1989* to other sales successes, such as Fleetwood Mac's *Rumours*, Bruce Springsteen's *Born in the U.S.A.*, and Celine Dion's *Falling into You*.

Caulfield, Keith. "Numbers: Swift's 'Woods' Bows." *Billboard* 128 (January 16, 2016), 56. A report on the upsurge in domestic streaming of Swift's "Out of the Woods" after she performed the song on *Dick Clark's New Year's Rockin' Eve with Ryan Seacrest*.

Caulfield, Keith and Gary Trust. "Swift Start." *Billboard* 124 (August 25, 2012), 4–5. A report on "We Are Never Ever Getting Back Together," which exhibits signs of being a radio hit.

Cefrey, Holly. *Taylor Swift*. New York: Rosen Central, 2011. A fairly brief biography targeted to readers ages 10 and up.

Chafkin, Max. "Tell Your Friends about Us." *Inc.* 32 (March 2010), 108–110. A report on celebrity endorsements on social media, including Swift's endorsement of a new Tasti D-Lite store in Nashville.

Chang, Bee-Shyuan. "Celebrity Endorsement." *New York Times* 160 (January 30, 2011), query.nytimes.com/gst/fullpage.html?res=9403E6D71F30F933A0575 2C0A9679D8B63. Accessed February 10, 2016. A report on pop artist Richard Phillips's London show "Most Wanted," in which he incorporated the images of a number of stars, including Swift.

Christman, Ed. "The Top 10 Stories of the Year: 4. Taylor Swift Sells 1 Million Albums." *Billboard* 122 (December 18, 2010), 24. A report on the success of *Speak Now* in an album market in which sales of one million albums in a debut week is now a rarity. Interestingly, 769k units were physical CDs and 278k were downloads.

Christman, Ed, Keith Caulfield, and William Gruger. "The Taylor Swift Playbook in 6 (Not So Easy) Steps." *Billboard* 126 (November 15, 2014), 13–14. An analysis of how *1989* managed to buck the trend of decreasing CD sales.

Click, Melissa, Hyunji Lee, and Holly Willson Holladay. "Making Monsters: Lady Gaga, Fan Identification, and Social Media." *Popular Music and Society* 36 (no. 3, 2013), 360–379.

Clover, Joshua. "Pop & Circumstance." *Nation* 296 (May 27, 2013), 37. A feature that revolves around the success of *Red* and Swift's importance.

Comentale, Edward P. "Dorking Out with Taylor and Kanye: Nerd Pop via Goffman and the Performance of Stigma." *Journal of Popular Music Studies* 28 (March 2016), 7–32. Taylor Swift is portrayed as a socially awkward musical nerd in this article. However, since the author also details the nerdiness of Buddy Holly and Elvis Costello in the same article, Swift is in good company.

Conniff, Kelly, Nolan Feeney, Lily Rothman, and Laura Stampler. "Pop Chart." *Time* 184 (July 21, 2014), 56–57. This article references Swift's *Wall Street Journal* op-ed piece in which she stated that songwriters need to work harder and make music that hits people "like an arrow through the heart."

Country Music Association. "Searchable CMA Awards Database," www.cmaworld.com/cma-awards/nominees/past-winners/?appSession=256137013016829. Accessed April 6, 2015.

Cullen, Shaun. "The Innocent and the Runaway: Kanye West, Taylor Swift, and the Cultural Politics of Racial Melodrama." *Journal of Popular Music Studies* 28 (March 2016), 33–50. A detailed study of the sociological implications of Kanye West's interruption of Swift's Video Music Awards acceptance speech and public reactions to it.

D'Addario, Daniel. "Taylor Swift Defends Albums as 'Art' at the American Music Awards." *Time.com* (November 24, 2014), time.com/3601721/taylor-swift -american-music-awards-speech-spotify/. Accessed February 16, 2016. A report on Swift's call to recognize albums as complete wholes in her speech at the American Music Awards.

D'Addario, Daniel. "Taylor Swift Silences 'Welcome to New York' Critics, Donates to Public Schools." *Time.com* (October 29, 2014), time.com/3546081/taylor -swift-welcome-to-new-york-public-schools/. Accessed February 17, 2016. A report on Swift's donation of all of the proceeds from "Welcome to New York" to the city's public schools. The article also mentions criticism that the song received for its "lifeless" portrayal of New York.

D'Addario, Daniel. "Taylor Swift's 'Welcome to New York' Is a New Kind of Equality Anthem." *Time.com* (October 21, 2014), time.com/3528687/ taylor-swift-welcome-to-new-york-1989-new-track-gay/. Accessed February 17,

2016. A report on Swift's "low-key" support of gay rights on *1989*'s opening track.

Dauphin, Chuck. "Taylor's Team." *Billboard* 123 (December 10, 2011), 28–30. A feature article on Swift's production and promotion team.

Deerwester, Jayme. "How Was Your Day?" *USA Today* (February 17, 2016), Life section, 1d. This article mentions Swift's warning to female artists at the 2016 Grammy Awards to make sure that no one undercuts them or takes credit for their work.

Dickey, Jack. "Apple Met Its Match—Swiftly." *Time* 186 (July 6, 2015), 37. Published in online format as Dickey, Jack. "How a 25-Year-Old Blogger Took Down Apple." *Time* (June 22, 2015), http://time.com/3930308/taylor-swift-apple/?iid=sr-link1. Accessed June 30, 2016. A report on Swift's open letter to Apple Music regarding compensation for artists during the streaming music provider's trial period.

Dickey, Jack. "Taylor Strikes a Chord." *Time* 184 (November 24, 2014), 42–49. An extensive profile of Swift with information about the album *1989*. Includes discussion of Swift's similarities to and differences from female singer-songwriters of the past.

Dickey, Jack. "Taylor Swift on *1989*, Spotify, Her Next Tour and Female Role Models." *Time.com* (November 13, 2014), time.com/3578249/taylor-swift-interview/. Accessed February 16, 2016. An essential feature article.

DiMatteo, Steve. "Track List for Taylor Swift's New Album Leaked." *Huffington Post* (October 13, 2015), www.huffingtonpost.com/steve-dimatteo/track-list-for-taylor-swi_b_8281980.html. Accessed June 3, 2016. A comic parody of Swift's penchant for turning her experiences with heartbreak into songs written in response to tabloid reports that Swift had broken up with boyfriend Calvin Harris.

Dobbins, Amanda. "Swift Justice." *New York* 45 (November 5, 2012), 65. A report on Swift's use of capital letters to deliver a "hidden" message that runs through the lyrics of *Red* in the CD booklet.

Dockterman, Eliana. "Watch Taylor Swift Praise Emma Watson for Her UN Feminism Speech." *Time.com* (September 30, 2014), time.com/3449450/taylor-swift-emma-watson-un-feminism-heforshe/. Accessed February 17, 2016.

Doerschuk, Bob. "Taylor Swift Goes Long." *CMA Close Up* 8 (2011), 16–17. The author provides some insights into Swift's world tour in support of *Speak Now*.

Doherty, Maggie. " 'If This Was a Movie.' " *Billboard* 123 (December 10, 2011), 77. A review of the single that describes it as more "age-appropriate" than some of her other works.

Dolan, Jon. "Taylor Crashes a Wedding." *Rolling Stone* 1116 (October 28, 2010), 62. A brief favorable review of "Speak Now." The author points out Swift's quotation of her earlier "she wears short skirts" melody from "You Belong with Me" in the current song.

Dolan, Jon. "Taylor's Great Pop Adventure." *Rolling Stone* 1169 (November 8, 2012), 66. A favorable review of *Red*, which describes the album as Swift's "Joni Mitchell-influenced maturity binge."

Dollard, Jennifer L. "Federal Judge Holds That Taylor Swift's Sick Beat Is All Hers." *Young Lawyer* 20 (Winter 2016), 3. A report on the dismissal of a copyright infringement lawsuit brought by Jesse Braham claiming that Swift had illegally used his lyrics for passages in "Shake It Off."

"Download This!" *People* 66 (November 8, 2006), 27–30. Swift's single, "The Outside," is included as one of the essential music downloads from *People*'s website.

Doyle, Patrick. "Swift's Bold New Direction." *Rolling Stone* 1165 (September 13, 2012), 17–18. A report on *Red* and Swift's desire to work with a variety of cowriters and producers on the various tracks. She mentions her love of R&B and hip hop.

Driscoll, Molly. "What Is the Taylor Swift Award? Singer Receives Prize at 2016 BMI Pop Awards." *Christian Science Monitor* (May 11, 2016), www.csmonitor.com/ The-Culture/Music/2016/0511/What-is-the-Taylor-Swift-Award-Singer-receives -prize-at-2016-BMI-Pop-Awards. Accessed June 2, 2016. A report on Broadcast Music, Inc.'s establishment of the Taylor Swift Award to recognize Swift's contributions to music and the seriousness with which she takes the rights of songwriters. Swift was the first winner of the award named after her.

Dyer, Elizabeth B. "Whitewashed African Film Sets: Taylor Swift's *Wildest Dreams* and *King Solomon's Mines.*" *African Studies Review* 59 (December 2016), 301–310. A study of Swift's somewhat controversial video for the song "Wildest Dreams," which, although set in Africa, uses a white cast. The author's contention seems to be that the Swift video tells more about the state of Hollywood filmmaking in the 1950s (the time period depicted) than it does about any biases that Swift and the video's writers and producers might have.

The Editors of CNN. "Bad Blood: Kim, Kanye and Taylor Clash on Social Media." *CNN.com* (July 18, 2016), http://www.cnn.com/videos/entertainment/ 2016/07/18/tds-taylor-swift-kardashian-feud.cnn. Accessed July 19, 2016. A report on the ongoing social media feud between Swift, Kim Kardashian, and Kanye West.

The Editors of *Instructor*. "Taylor Swift Webcast." *Instructor* 122 (Fall 2012), 10. A brief report on an October 24, 2012, live webcast by Swift on the power of reading.

The Editors of *International Musician*. "Taylor Swift Donates to Aid Flood Victims." *International Musician* 114 (September 2016), 10. A report on Swift's donation to help with flood relief in Louisiana.

The Editors of *New Scientist*. "Taylor Shakes off Apple." *New Scientist* 226 (June 27, 2015). A brief report on Swift's open letter regarding Apple's decision not to pay royalties for free streaming during the three-month trial period for users of Apple Music. Apple reversed its decision in the wake of Swift's Internet-posted open letter.

The Editors of *Rolling Stone*. "Buy These Now." *Rolling Stone* 1066 (November 27, 2008), 121. A brief favorable review of *Fearless*.

The Editors of *Scholastic Scope*. "Taylor Swift." *Scholastic Scope* 59 (January 10, 2011), 19. A brief profile of the singer-songwriter who was "once bullied and ignored" and "is now a worldwide superstar."

The Editors of *Scholastic Scope*. "Taylor Writes the Songs." *Scholastic Scope* 57 (February 2, 2009), 4. A brief profile of Swift and the fact that many of her songs concerned real life in an American high school.

The Editors of *Time*. "10 Questions." *Time* 173 (May 4, 2009), 4. Various fans submitted questions to Swift who revealed that most of the "songs that I write end up being finished in 30 minutes or less." She also discusses her love of the band Def Leppard and her desire to sing duets with Taylor Hanson.

Eells, Josh. "John Mayer's Regrets." *Rolling Stone* 1159 (June 21, 2012), 48–53. Concerning Swift's song "Dear John," Mayer reports that Swift released the song without warning him ahead of time.

Eells, Josh. "The Reinvention of Taylor Swift." *Rolling Stone* 1218 (September 25, 2014), 38+, http://www.rollingstone.com/music/features/taylor-swift-1989-cover-story-20140908. Accessed March 21, 2017. A feature article on Swift's move to New York City, her decision to remain single, the media attention that surrounds her, and her move from country music to dance-oriented pop music on *1989*.

Elliott, Stuart. "Keds Enlists Taylor Swift to Transmit Girl Power." *New York Times* 162 (January 24, 2013), www.nytimes.com/2013/01/24/business/media/keds-campaign-features-taylor-swift.html. Accessed February 15, 2016. A report on Keds' enlistment of Swift to promote its shoes.

Erlewine, Stephen Thomas. "*1989*." All Music Guide, www.allmusic.com/album/1989-mw0002726289. Accessed April 22, 2016. A somewhat mixed review of *1989*.

Feeney, Nolan. "Taylor Swift's 'Welcome to New York' Is the Musical Equivalent of a Peppermint Latte." *Time.com* (October 20, 2014), time.com/3525590/taylor-swift-welcome-to-new-york-full/. Accessed February 17, 2016. A brief review that focuses on the song's connections to 1980s dance styles.

Feeney, Nolan. " 'Wildest Dreams' Director Defends Taylor Swift Video against Whitewashing." *Time.com* (September 2, 2015), time.com/4020783/taylor-swift-wildest-dreams-director-defends-controversy/. Accessed February 17, 2016. A report on Joseph Kahn's defense of Swift's "Wildest Dreams" video, which features a largely white cast, although it is set in Africa. The video is based on classic films such as *The African Queen* and *Out of Africa*, movies with nearly all-white casts and crews.

Fields, Jackie. "Shimmering Eyes." *People* 72 (December 21, 2009), 130. A brief report on the use of shimmering eye makeup by artists such as Swift and Rihanna.

Finan, Eileen. "Country's Teen Queen." *People* 67 (May 21, 2007), 122. A profile of Swift.

Frehsée, Nicole. "Taylor Swift's N.Y. Lovefest." *Rolling Stone* 1087 (September 17, 2009), 22. A report on Swift's recent concert in New York's Madison Square Garden.

Frere-Jones, Sasha. "Prodigy." *New Yorker* 84 (November 10, 2008), 86–87. A favorable review of Swift's debut album that mentions the ageless quality of Swift's compositions.

Freydkin, Donna and Alison Maxwell. "Fashion Forward." *USA Today* (December 24, 2008), Life section, 2d. A brief report on the clothing that Swift wore on the *Late Show with David Letterman*.

Frisch, Aaron. *Taylor Swift*. Mankato, MN: Creative Education, 2013. A short children's book on Swift and her music.

Frizell, Sam. "Taylor Swift Finally Explains Why She's a Feminist and How Lena Dunham Helped." *Time.com* (August 25, 2014), time.com/3165825/taylor-swift-feminist-lena-dunham/. Accessed February 16, 2016. A brief article on Swift's brand of feminism, a view that revolves around equality.

Gallo, Phil. "Primary Colors." *Billboard* 124 (October 27, 2012), 12–15. A lengthy preview of *Red*. Swift is quoted as saying that the various genres and the use of a variety of track producers were necessitated by the fact that the emotional content of the lyrics of each song drove the musical genre and production style more than on any of her previous albums.

Gallo, Phil. "The Twilight of 'Twilight.' " *Billboard* 124 (December 22, 2012), 34. A report on the soundtrack for *The Hunger Games,* to which Swift contributed.

Ganz, Caryn. "Taylor Swift." *Rolling Stone* 1062 (October 2, 2008), 34. A favorable review of *Fearless.*

Gardner, Elysa. "Taylor Swift Hits All the Right Words." *USA Today* (November 11, 2008), 5d. A favorable review of *Fearless.*

Gardner, Elysa. "When Swift Speaks, Listen." *USA Today* (October 22, 2010), Life section, 2d. A favorable review of *Speak Now,* an album that represents Swift "becoming an adult." The reviewer suggests skipping the track "Better than Revenge."

Geffen, Sasha. "Taylor Swift Snapped Selfies and Shared Smiles with Fans Battling Cancer." *MTV News* (July 12, 2016), http://www.mtv.com/news/2903825/taylor-swift-childrens-hospital-australia/. Accessed July 12, 2016.

Gibson, Megan. "Taylor Swift Says Other Artists Thanked Her for Pulling Her Music from Spotify." *Time.com* (December 18, 2014), time.com/3639542/taylor-swift-spotify-thank-you/. Accessed February 17, 2016. A brief report on Swift's battle for artists' royalties with the streaming audio service Spotify.

Gleason, Holly. "Taylor Swift Not 'Just a Girl' Anymore." *CMA Close Up* (February–March 2008), 20–21. An article on Swift's career to date.

Goulet, Matt. "What Taylor Swift Is Doing to the Women." *Esquire* 160 (October 2013), 102.

Graham, Jefferson. "App Makes It a Cinch to Add Backup Band." *USA Today* (January 21, 2016), Money section, 3b. This report on the Music Memos app for Apple devices mentions that Swift used the company's earlier Voice Memos app to record song demos, three of which were included on *1989.*

Greenblatt, Leah. " 'Love Story.' " *Entertainment Weekly* 1014 (October 3, 2008), 76. A favorable review of Swift's single "Love Story."

Greenblatt, Leah. "*Speak Now.*" *Entertainment Weekly* 1127 (November 5, 2010), 68. A favorable review of the album that praises Swift's ability to tell stories in her songs.

Greenblatt, Leah. "Taylor Swift." *Entertainment Weekly* 1020 (November 14, 2008), 72. A generally favorable review of *Fearless.*

Grigoriadis, Vanessa. "The Very Pink, Very Perfect Life of Taylor Swift." *Rolling Stone* 1073 (March 5, 2009), 44–51. A profile of Swift's day-to-day life but with the unexpected revelation that she is interested in Jackson Pollock's style of art.

Grossman, Samantha. "Taylor Swift Just Donated $15,000 to the Firefighter Who Saved His Own Family." *Time.com* (June 12, 2015), time.com/3918995/taylor-swift-firefighter-donation/. Accessed May 19, 2016. A report on Swift's verified donation.

Grossman, Samantha. "Watch Taylor Swift Sing, Dance and Play Air Hockey with a Young Cancer Patient." *Time.com* (August 4, 2014), time.com/3079471/watch-taylor-swift-sing-dance-and-play-air-hockey-with-a-young-cancer-patient/. Accessed February 18, 2016. Includes a link to a video of Swift interacting with her fan who was undergoing treatment for cancer.

Hajdu, David. "Pop Women." *New Republic* 240 (February 4, 2009), 27–30. The author questions Swift's understanding of the real life of junior high and high school students, because she deals so much with romance and not with sex in her songs.

Hampp, Andrew. "Beyond Branding." *Billboard* 123 (December 10, 2011), 32. A report on Swift's connections to Target, CoverGirl, Sony Electronics, Wal-Mart, and other companies.

Hampp, Andrew. " 'I Knew You Were Trouble.' " *Billboard* 124 (December 8, 2012), 81. A favorable review of the singer who "has all along been a pop star who happens to appeal to country audiences—never the other way around."

Hampp, Andrew and Phil Gallo. "Seeing *Red*." *Billboard* 124 (October 27, 2012), 15. A report on how branding—and Swift's deals with Sony, Target, Papa John's, Walgreen's, etc.—could enable *Red* to match the strong sales of *Speak Now*.

Hasty, Katie. "Swift's Un-Swift Climb." *Billboard* 119 (August 4, 2007), 9. This brief report on Taylor Swift includes a comment from Becky Brenner, program director of radio station KMPS regarding the importance of MySpace in Swift's promotion.

Hau, Louis, Ed Christman, and Craig Marks. "The Only Girl in the World." *Billboard* 122 (November 13, 2010), 5. A report on the album *Speak Now* that emphasizes Swift's intergenerational crossover appeal.

Herdon, Jessica. "*Fearless*." *People* 70 (November 7, 2008), 45. A favorable review of *Fearless*.

Herrera, Monica. "*Hunger Games* LP Recruits All-Stars." *Rolling Stone* 1153 (March 29, 2012), 19–20. A report on *The Hunger Games*, for which Swift contributed "Safe & Sound" and "Eyes Open," which revolve around fictional characters.

Hiatt, Brian. "Taylor in Wonderland." *Rolling Stone* 1168 (October 25, 2012), 34+. A feature article on Swift that focuses on her daily life on the road.

Hinckley, Story. "Taylor Swift's $250,000 Donation to Kesha: An Act of Feminism?" *Christian Science Monitor* (February 22, 2016), www.csmonitor.com/USA/Society/2016/0222/Taylor-Swift-s-250-000-donation-to-Kesha-An-act-of-feminism-video. Accessed February 23, 2016.

Hoffman, Ashley. "These Fake Taylor Swift Songs about the Kanye West-Kim Kardashian Feud Are Perfect." *Time.com* (July 25, 2016), http://time.com/4419293/taylor-swift-kanye-west-kim-kardashian-song-parody/. Accessed February 1, 2017. A report on a YouTube.com post of songs that parody the West/Kardashian/Swift feud.

Iannacci, Elio. " 'Everyone I Know Has Had Fair Warning!' " *Maclean's* 123 (November 8, 2010), 117. Swift discusses her tendency to write songs about real-life experiences and glossing over very little. The article also discusses "various LGBT-friendly blogs . . . adopting Swift's 'Mean' as an anti-bullying anthem."

Iasimone, Ashley. "Taylor Swift Shares the Stories Behind 'Out of the Woods' and 'I Know Places.' " *Billboard* (October 11, 2015), www.billboard.com/articles/columns/pop-shop/6722969/taylor-swift-out-of-the-woods-i-know-places-stories-grammy-pro. Accessed May 6, 2016. A brief report on the inspirations for the two tracks from the album *1989*.

Itzkoff, Dave. "Defending Taylor Swift." *New York Times* 159 (February 5, 2010), 5. A report on Big Machine Records president Scott Borchetta's defense of Swift as "the undisputed best communicator that we've got," despite the fact that her vocal performance at the Grammy Awards was not as technically polished as it might have been.

Itzkoff, Dave. "It's Taylor Swift in New Pop-Art Portraits." *New York Times* 160 (December 11, 2010), 2. A report that the famous pop artist Peter Max created a series of paintings based on Swift's album covers.

James, Rachel McCarthy. "Swift Judgment." *Bitch Magazine: Feminist Response to Pop Culture* 50 (Spring 2011), 15–21. A feature-length analytical article on Swift's public image and her work from a feminist perspective. Although the author sees much evidence of Swift's perpetuation of "gender boundaries," she writes that "Sparks Fly" and "Mean" "take a more complex look at how to negotiate the no-win arena of double standards all women face."

Jessen, Wade. "Sixth Week Puts Swift in Elite Company." *Billboard* 120 (January 26, 2008), 75. According to this article, the fact that "Our Song" has been No. 1 on the country charts for six weeks in a row makes Swift only the third female artist ever to achieve that feat.

Johnston, Lisa. "A Pop Princess and Her Fight for Fairness." *TWICE: This Week in Consumer Electronics* 30 (December 21, 2015), 26. A brief report on Swift's battles with Spotify and Apple Music regarding compensation for artists.

Johnston, Maura. "Taylor Swift." *New York Times Magazine* (September 8, 2013), 32. A feature article on Swift.

Jones, Chris. "(Who the F#@& Is) Taylor Swift." *Esquire* 151 (April 2009), 78. The author confesses that he was "the last man on earth to have never heard a Taylor Swift song." He also confesses his attraction to the song "Love Story."

Junod, Tom. "Bow Down." *Esquire* 163 (June/July 2015), 22–24. The performance styles and the pop cultural impact of Swift and Beyoncé are the subjects of this article.

Kedmey, Dan. "Spotify CEO 'Really Frustrated' with Taylor Swift." *Time.com* (November 11, 2014), time.com/3578098/taylor-swift-spotify-ceo/. Accessed February 16, 2016. A report on Spotify's reaction to Swift pulling the vast majority of her recordings from the streaming audio service.

Kirby, Kip. "Taylor Swift Sees *Red* and Stays Country." *CMA Close Up* (August–September 2013), 16–19. A report on Swift's popularity and her continuing ties to country music, despite the pop style of *Red*.

Knopper, Steve. "YouTube vs. the Music Industry." *Rolling Stone* 1268 (August 25, 2016), 22–23. A report on the existence of YouTube channels with, in some cases, hundreds of unauthorized recordings of Taylor Swift's music and those of other prominent pop artists.

Knowles, David. "*Fearless*." *Maverick* 79 (February 2009), 74–75. A generally favorable review of Swift's second album. The author praises her voice but notes that the musical style and lyrical foci of Swift's lyrics seem to be a bit overly tied to her age group.

Lang, Cady. "Watch Dave Grohl Tell You about the Time He Got High at Paul McCartney's House and Taylor Swift Saved Him." *Time.com* (June 27, 2016), http://time.com/4382198/taylor-swift-dave-grohl-paul-mccartney/. Accessed February 1, 2017. A report on the Foo Fighters' Dave Grohl being bailed out by Taylor Swift at a party at Paul McCartney's house. When Grohl was unable to play a song at McCartney's urging, Swift jumped in and performed.

Lansky, Sam. "Paradigm Swift." *Time* 184 (November 3, 2014), 55. A brief, favorable review of *1989* that focuses on Swift's move away from country music as well as increasing lyrical maturity.

Leight, Elias. "Taylor Swift's Samizdat Songwriting: An Expert Weighs In." *Billboard* 128 (December 17, 2016), 44. A brief article in which the songwriter Busbee discusses songs that Swift wrote for other artists in 2016: "This Is What You Came For" and "Better Man."

Lendino, Jamie. "Why Music Should Not Be Free." *PC Magazine* (December 2014), 29–32. Swift's support of royalties for songwriters and performers is included in this article.

Light, Alan. "Taylor Swift." *Billboard* 126 (December 13, 2014), 64–71. A feature interview with Swift that focuses on Swift's move to New York City, her change from country music to more mainstream dance-based pop, and other topics.

Linshi, Jack. "Here's Why Taylor Swift Pulled Her Music from Spotify." *Time.com* (November 4, 2014), time.com/3554468/why-taylor-swift-spotify/. Accessed February 16, 2016. A report on the controversy over Spotify's royalty payments to artists.

Lipshutz, Jason. "Taylor Swift, 'Shake It Off.' " *Billboard* 126 (August 30, 2014), 66. A favorable review.

Lipshutz, Jason. " 'We Are Never Getting Back Together.' " *Billboard* 124 (September 1, 2012), 37. A brief favorable review of the single.

Liss, Sarah. "Who, Me? Famous?" *Maclean's* 127 (November 3, 2014), 52–54. A report on the social image of Swift. As Swift has become increasingly famous, some of her appeal as a regular, everyday person has been lost. However, the author counterpoints Beyoncé's diva-ness with Swift's everyday person-ness.

Llen, Bob. "Swift's *Red* Tour Takes First No. 1." *Billboard* 125 (April 27, 2013), 67. A brief report on the sales success of Swift's concert tour in support of *Red*.

Luckerson, Victor. "Why Only Taylor Swift Could Leave Spotify." *Time* (November 5, 2014), time.com/3556721/taylor-swift-spotify-1989/. Accessed February 17, 2016. According to Luckerson, Swift could pull her music out of the streaming music service Spotify because "she operates on a different plan from the rest of the music biz."

Macsai, Dan. "Taylor Swift." *Time* 180 (October 29, 2012), 64. A profile of Swift.

Maerz, Melissa. "Safe & Sound." *Entertainment Weekly* 1188 (January 6, 2012), 73. A brief favorable review of "Safe & Sound."

Maerz, Melissa. "Taylor Swift." *Entertainment Weekly* 1230 (October 26, 2012), 73–74. A generally favorable review of *Red*.

Mansfield, Brian. "Not All Boys Make Her Cry." *USA Today* (August 8, 2008), Life section, 11d. A brief report on Swift widening her lyrical focal points on *Fearless*.

Mansfield, Brian. "On the Verge." *USA Today* (November 21, 2006), Life section, 5d. A brief report on Swift's activities in the wake of the success of "Tim McGraw." Swift also describes writing the song in her high school math class. She also acknowledged coding the name of the boy who inspired "Should've Said No" into the liner notes of her debut CD.

Mansfield, Brian. "*Red* Puts Swift in Rarefied Company." *USA Today* (October 31, 2012), Life section, 3d. This report on the high sales success of the album quotes Yahoo Music writer Chris Willman as calling Swift "the voice of her generation."

Mansfield, Brian. "Taylor Learns to 'Speak Now'." *USA Today* (October 22, 2010), Life section, 1d. A profile of Swift at the time of the release of *Speak Now*. The article focuses on the growing maturity of Swift's lyrics.

Mansfield, Brian. "Taylor Swift's *Red* Marks Change of Pace." *USA Today* (October 18, 2012), Life section, 1d. A feature article on *Red* and its not-entirely-successful reception with the country music audience.

Markowitz, Adam. "Congratulations, Taylor Swift!" *Entertainment Weekly* 1078 (December 4, 2009), 24. A brief report on, among other things, Swift's hosting of NBC's *Saturday Night Live.*

Markowitz, Adam. "Taylor Swift." *Entertainment Weekly* 1082/1083 (December 25, 2009), 52–53. A profile of Swift and report on *Fearless.*

Markowitz, Adam. "Taylor Swift." *Entertainment Weekly* 1335 (October 31, 2014), 62–63. A somewhat mixed review of *1989.* The writer finds that the arrangements and the lyrics are too difficult to define.

Marquina, Sierra. "Taylor Swift, Calvin Harris Split: 'Love Is Dead' and More of the Best Internet Reactions." *US Magazine* (June 1, 2016), www.usmagazine .com/celebrity-news/news/taylor-swift-calvin-harris-split-best-internet-reactions -w208539. Accessed June 3, 2016.

Martin, Justin D. "Beyoncé, Lady Gaga, Katy Perry, Taylor Swift Sing a New Message of Girl Power." *Christian Science Monitor* (November 25, 2011), www .csmonitor.com/Commentary/Opinion/2011/1125/Beyonce-Lady-Gaga-Katy -Perry-Taylor-Swift-sing-a-new-message-of-girl-power. Accessed February 10, 2016. A report on the author's experience listening to hits by female artists on the radio during an extended driving trip. Swift and the others expressed female empowerment in many of their songs.

Martin, Peter. "Other Women We Love." *Esquire* 158 (November 2012), 26–28. A brief interview.

Marwick, Alice and danah boyd. "To See and Be Seen: Celebrity Practice on Twitter." *Convergence: The International Journal of Research into New Media Technologies* 17 (no. 2, 2011), 139–158. Although this article deals with other celebrities' use of Twitter in various forms of "celebrity management," some of the findings pertain to Swift's use of social media.

McClusky, Megan. "Taylor Swift and Calvin Harris' Vacation Photos Are Annoyingly Perfect." *Time.com* (March 16, 2016), time.com/4261061/taylor-swift-calvin -harris-vacation/?iid=sr-link1. Accessed June 2, 2016.

McIntyre, Samantha. "Mall Chic!" *People* 71 (June 22, 2009), 134–136. A brief report on celebrities who wear fashions purchased at mall stores. Swift's dress is from French Connection.

McKinley, James C., Jr. "Swift Giving $4 Million to Hall of Fame and Museum." *New York Times* 161 (May 18, 2012), query.nytimes.com/gst/fullpage.html? res=9F04E7D7143CF93BA25756C0A9649D8B63. Accessed February 12, 2016. A report on Swift's donation of $4 million to Nashville's County Music Hall of Fame and Museum.

Meyer, Philip N. "What Adele and Taylor Swift Can Teach You about Finding Justice." *ABA Journal* (June 2016), 25. A report on how the ideas of justice and retribution are played out in the songs of Adele and Swift.

Mossman, Kate. "Tweenage Dreams." *New Statesman* 143 (February 7, 2014), 54–55. A favorable review of a Swift performance in London.

Murray, Nick. "Taylor Swift." *Rolling Stone* 1236 (June 4, 2015), 16. A brief article about the technical side of Swift's *1989* tour, including how her touring band was being taught by producer Max Martin to reproduce the sound of the album.

Neal, Chris. "Taylor Swift." *Performing Songwriter* 16 (November 2008), 20. A brief interview with Swift about the inspiration for her songs and her writing techniques.

Newkey-Burden, Chas. *Taylor Swift: The Whole Story.* New York: HarperCollins, 2014. A biography for readers 11 years old and up.

Newman, Jason. "Taylor Swift Donates $250,000 to Kesha after Court Ruling." *Rolling Stone* (February 22, 2016) www.rollingstone.com/music/news/taylor-swift -donates-250-000-to-kesha-after-court-ruling-20160222. Accessed June 2, 2016. A brief report on Swift's donation to Kesha after a court ruled against her in Kesha's lawsuit against Sony and producer Dr. Luke.

Nicks, Stevie. "The 2010 *Time* 100: Taylor Swift." *Time.com* (April 29, 2010), content.time.com/time/specials/packages/article/ 0,28804,1984685_1984940_1985536,00.html. Accessed February 29, 2016. A brief commentary about Swift's importance as a country-pop-rock singer-songwriter written by the well-known member of Fleetwood Mac.

Novak, Ralph. "Taylor Swift." *People* 66 (November 20, 2006), 49. A brief mixed review of *Taylor Swift*, in which the author refers to Swift as "Nashville's answer to Britney Spears."

Parker, Jill. *Tay: The Taylor Swift Story.* Beverly Hills, CA: Sole Books, 2015. A biography.

Peoples, Glenn. "Swift's Streaming Staredown." *Billboard* 126 (November 22, 2014), 12. A report on Swift pulling all of her songs but one from Spotify's streaming audio service.

Peppas, Lynn. *Taylor Swift.* New York: Crabtree Publishing, 2011. A brief biography written for 8–11-year-olds.

Perone, James E. "Taylor Swift: *Fearless* (2008)." In Perone, James E., ed. *The Album: A Guide to Pop Music's Most Provocative, Influential, and Important Creations,* vol. 4. Santa Barbara, CA: Praeger Publishers, 2012, 185–189.

Perry, Simon and Eileen Finan. "Queen of Her Own Heart." *People* 82 (October 20, 2014), 64–68. A brief report on Swift's motivations behind her album *1989.*

Pietroluongo, Silvio. "Swift's Bonus Track Bounty." *Billboard* 121 (November 14, 2009), 42. A brief report that as of the publication date Swift had eight songs on the Hot 100 Songs chart, "the most by any female artist in the chart's history."

Price, Deborah Evans. " 'Love Story.' " *Billboard* 120 (October 11, 2008), 50. A favorable review of the single. According to Evans, "Country's own love affair with Swift will only gain momentum with this 'Story'."

Price, Deborah Evans. " 'Mine.' " *Billboard* 122 (August 21, 2010), 36. A favorable review of "Mine," in which the author notes the increased presence of "lyrical substance" in Swift's work.

Price, Deborah Evans. " 'Our Song.' " *Billboard* 119 (September 29, 2007), 54. A highly favorable review of the single.

Price, Deborah Evans. " 'Picture to Burn.' " *Billboard* 120 (February 23, 2008), 52. A favorable review of the single, which features a "sing-along chorus that you won't be able to dismiss from your memory bank."

Price, Deborah Evans. " 'Teardrops on My Guitar.' " *Billboard* 119 (March 17, 2007), 52. A favorable review of "Teardrops on My Guitar."

Queenan, Joe. "In Awe of Taylor Swift—but Enough!" *Wall Street Journal* 256 (December 11, 2010), Eastern Edition, C11. A report and commentary on the huge amount of media attention that is paid to Swift.

Raab, Scott. "ESQ&A." *Esquire* 162 (November 2014), 37–41. An interview with Swift on coverage of her personal life by the media, her song "Shake It Off," and her working habits.

Reusser, Kayleen. *Day by Day with Taylor Swift.* Hockessin, DE: Mitchell Lane Publishers, 2010. A brief biographical book aimed at elementary school-aged children.

Robinson, Will. "Taylor Swift's 'Tim McGraw' Turns 10." *Entertainment Weekly* 1420 (June 20, 2016), 58. A brief report on the anniversary of the release of Swift's single "Tim McGraw," the song that launched her career.

Roland, Tom. "Country Logs On." *Billboard* 123 (December 17, 2011), 40. A report on the growing trend of young country artists, including Swift, connecting with their fans and selling their music through social media.

Roland, Tom. "Days of Thunder." *Billboard* 123 (September 24, 2011), 20–25. A feature article on Scott Borchetta, the head of Big Machine Records, Swift's label.

Roland, Tom. "How Sparks Fly." *Billboard* 123 (December 10, 2011), 22–26. A feature on Swift at the conclusion of her world tour, becoming No. 7 on the list of all-time bestselling female vocalists (based on most Hot 100 hits), her donations of over $1 million to charity in the past year, and her selection as *Billboard*'s Woman of the Year, the youngest recipient of the honor.

Roland, Tom. "Princess Superstar." *Billboard* 122 (October 23, 2010), 18–21. A feature article on *Speak Now* and the new maturity that the album represents for Swift as a singer and as a songwriter. The article also focuses on Swift's ability to cross generational boundaries in her appeal.

Rosen, Jody. "Country's Most Precocious Teen Princess Lets the World Read Her Diary." *Rolling Stone* 1065 (November 13, 2008), 89–90. A highly favorable review of Swift's debut album.

Rosen, Jody. "Taylor Swift Is the Reigning Queen of Pop." *New York* 46 (November 25, 2013), 44+. A feature article on Swift's career success.

Rosen, Jody. "Taylor's Hilarious Breakup Postmortem." *Rolling Stone* 1165 (September 13, 2012), 81. A favorable review of "We Are Never Ever Getting Back Together." Rosen takes special delight in "the most sublime spoken-word interlude in pop since Barry White died."

Ryan, Patrick and Brian Mansfield. "Taylor Swift Is a Country Dweller No More." *USA Today* (August 19, 2014), Life section, 1d. A report on the pop music nature of *1989*.

Samuels, Kathy, Brian Goldner, Stephen Davis, and Todd Cassetty, executive producers. *Taylor Swift: The Journey to Fearless.* Los Angeles, CA: Shout Factory SF12933. DVD Video. In addition to live performances of "You Belong with Me," "Tim McGraw," "Fifteen," "Teardrops on My Guitar," "Our Song," "Today Was a Fairytale," "Love Story," "Hey Stephen," "Tell Me Why," "Fearless," "Forever & Always," "Picture to Burn," and "Should've Said No," this 2-1/2-hour video includes a significant amount of biographical information and information on the inspirations for Swift's songs.

Saxton, Emily. "*Red.*" *Maverick* 118 (January–February 2013), 95. A favorable review that describes the album as "a distinct leap into musical (and songwriting) maturity."

Saxton, Emily. "Taylor Swift." *Maverick* 117 (November/December 2012), 58–63. A feature article on Swift and her work as of November 2012.

Scaggs, Austin. "Taylor Swift." *Rolling Stone* 1066 (November 27, 2008), 38. A brief interview with Swift on a variety of subjects, including her singing of the U.S. national anthem.

Scaggs, Austin. "Taylor Swift." *Rolling Stone* 1097 (February 4, 2010), 26. A brief interview.

Scaggs, Austin. "Taylor Swift." *Rolling Stone* 1117 (November 11, 2010), 30. A brief interview in which Swift discusses writing "Innocent" in response to her encounter with Kanye West at the Video Music Awards program, the source of inspiration for some of her other compositions, her interest in Japanese cooking, and her interest in the music of Faith Hill and other artists.

Scaggs, Austin. "Taylor Swift." *Rolling Stone* 1137 (August 18, 2011), 28. A brief interview with Swift.

Setoodeh, Ramin. "What Makes Taylor Tick." *Newsweek* 160 (October 29, 2012), 54. A brief interview.

Sheffield, Rob. "America's Sweetheart Edges toward Adulthood on Her Best Disc Yet." *Rolling Stone* 1117 (November 11, 2010), 69–70. A highly favorable review of *Speak Now*. Sheffield writes that there are no older artists than Swift who are making better pop records than she is.

Shmurda, Bobby. "I Taught Taylor Swift How to Dance." *Entertainment Weekly* 1341 (December 12, 2014), 28. Shmurda discusses his Shmoney Dance and seeing artists such as Swift using it in their live performances.

Shriver, Jerry. "Taylor Swift Has a Glow on *Red*." *USA Today* (October 22, 2012), Life section, 1d. A largely favorable review, which focuses on Swift's increasing lyrical maturity. The author notes, however, that "Sad, Beautiful, Tragic" is less successful than other tracks.

Silsby, Zoe. "Homecoming." *America* 214 (January 4, 2016), 31–32. The author, a freshman at Boston College, tells of how she finds references to her Roman Catholic faith in unexpected places and points to Swift's lyrics "You can hear it in the silence, you can feel it on the way home, you can see it with the lights out" as a metaphor for faith.

Sisario, Ben. "Chief Defends Spotify after Snub by Pop Star." *New York Times* 164 (November 12, 2014), www.nytimes.com/2014/11/12/business/media/taylor-swifts-stand-on-royalties-draws-a-rebuttal-from-spotify.html?_r=0. Accessed February 17, 2016. A report that Spotify's CEO Daniel Ek issued a statement about the amount of royalties the streaming audio service had paid to artists. This was in response to Taylor Swift's criticism of Spotify and her pulling her music from the service.

Sisario, Ben. "Taylor Swift Maximizes Use of Social Media in Release of New Album." *New York Times* 163 (August 19, 2014), www.nytimes.com/2014/08/19/business/media/taylor-swift-maximizes-use-of-social-media-in-release-of-new-album.html?_r=0. Accessed February 16, 2016. A report on Yahoo's live streaming and other social media releases of material from *1989*.

Smith, Ethan. "Taylor Swift Album Fast Out of the Gate." *Wall Street Journal* 260 (October 30, 2012), Eastern Edition, B9. A report on the sales of *Red*, which were bolstered by Swift's sponsorship deals.

Stack, Tim. "Kanye Steals the Spotlight." *Entertainment Weekly* 1067 (September 25, 2009), 11–13. A report on Kanye West's interruption of Swift's acceptance speech for Best Female Video at the MTV video awards program. The article reports on Katie Perry's tweet "Fuck U Kanye" and U.S. president Barack Obama's characterization of West as an "asshole."

Stack, Tim. "3. Taylor Swift." *Entertainment Weekly* 1134/1135 (December 24, 2010), 112. According to this review of "Back to December," "Swift never sounded more adult than on this tune."

Stark, George. "Taylor Swift and Nicki Minaj Clash on Twitter over MTV VMA Nominations." *Time.com* (July 22, 2015), time.com/3967305/taylor-swift-nicki-minaj-twitter/. Accessed February 17, 2016. A report on the Swift-Minaj feud on Twitter.

Strecker, Erin. "Remember When Taylor Swift Shined as *Saturday Night Live Host*?" *Billboard* (January 2, 2015), http://www.billboard.com/articles/columns/pop-shop/6429325/taylor-swift-saturday-night-live-host-flashback. Accessed June 8, 2016.

Strecker, Erin. "Taylor Swift Shocks Fans in New 'Shake It Off' Outtakes Video." *Billboard* (October 9, 2014), www.billboard.com/articles/6281279/taylor-swift-shake-it-off-outtakes-video. Accessed May 3, 2016.

Sutherland, Mark. "It Never Goes Out of Style: Inside *1989*'s Slowburning UK Success." *Music Week* (February 15, 2016), 3. A report on the sales success of *1989* in the United Kingdom, in which the album had sold over a million copies.

Swift, Taylor. "Best Country Duo." *Rolling Stone* 1129 (April 28, 2011), 62. A brief sound-bite-sized blurb in which Swift praises the duo John Paul White and Joy Williams.

Swift, Taylor. "It's Too Soon to Write Off the Album." *Wall Street Journal* 264 (July 8, 2014), Eastern Edition, R10. Also available as Swift, Taylor. "For Taylor Swift the Future of Music Is a Love Story." *Wall Street Journal* (July 7, 2014), www.wsj.com/articles/for-taylor-swift-the-future-of-music-is-a-love-story-1404763219. Accessed May 19, 2016. An op-ed piece in which Swift expresses her concerns with streaming audio services, particularly with their lack of payment, or low payment, of royalties to artists. She also discusses the emotional connection between artists and their fans.

Tannenbaum, Rob. "4 Ways Taylor Swift Changed Nashville." *Billboard* 126 (December 13, 2014), 71. According to the author, Swift's success led to younger country artists being signed, greater expectations that country singers write their own songs, a closer connection between country and pop, and a realization in the music industry of the importance of social media.

Tarr, Greg. "Sony Kicks off 'Make.Believe' with Cyber-Shot Program." *TWICE: This Week in Consumer Electronics* 25 (May 3, 2010), 25. A report on Sony's digital camera marketing campaign, which includes Swift as part of the advertising campaign.

Taylor, Chuck. " 'Tears on My Guitar.' " *Billboard* 120 (January 12, 2008), 40. A favorable review of the single, which is characterized as "a beautiful mainstream intro to an artist whose rise is ably exemplified by her last name."

Truitt, Brian. "Lamar and Swift Have That Golden Touch." *USA Today* (February 16, 2016), Life section, 1d. A report on the winners at the 2016 Grammy Awards.

Trust, Gary. "Holding On." *Billboard* 121 (November 7, 2009), 62. A report on Swift's debut album remaining in the *Billboard* 200 for 157 consecutive weeks, "the longest-running album on the chart this decade since 2000."

Trust, Gary. "Lucky 13." *Billboard* 123 (May 14, 2011), 32. A brief report on "Mean" being Swift's string of thirteen Top 10 country singles in a row, which matches Carrie Underwood's record.

Trust, Gary. "Swift Makes Crossover History." *Billboard* 121 (October 3, 2009), 66. A report on the fact that "You Belong with Me" was the first country song to reach the top of the Hot 100 Airplay charts, since a new data collection system started being used in 1990.

Tucker, Ken. "*Fearless*." *Billboard* 120 (November 15, 2008), 41. A favorable review of *Fearless* that includes commentary on Swift's wide demographic appeal.

Tucker, Ken. "Indies on the Rise." *Billboard* 119 (November 17, 2007), 8. A report on the recent success of artists such as Swift, who are not signed to major labels.

Tucker, Ken. "MySpace Generation." *Billboard* 119 (April 28, 2007), 9. A report on the use of social media—in particular Myspace.com and YouTube.com—by artists such as Swift and Sugarland.

Tucker, Ken. "Nashville Boots Up." *Billboard* 120 (March 22, 2008), 22–26. Includes information on Swift's use of MySpace to stay in touch with fans and her more than 650,000 MySpace "friends."

Tucker, Ken. "Swift Success." *Billboard* 120 (December 20, 2008), 80. According to this article, Swift was ranked No. 1 on the magazine's recap of the bestselling country artists of 2008.

Tucker, Ken. "Taylor Swift Goes Global." *Billboard* 120 (October 25, 2008), 22–25. A feature article on Swift, her appeal to a wide age range, her use of social media to connect with her friends, and her plans for an international concert tour.

Vick, Megan. " 'Back to December.' " *Billboard* 123 (January 8, 2011), 49. According to this favorable review of the single, the song "displays [Swift's] lyrical growth."

Vokes-Dudgeon, Sophie. "Taylor Swift Grants Terminally Ill 4-Year-Old's Final Wish, Talks via FaceTime with Cancer Patient." *US Magazine* (March 4, 2015), www.usmagazine.com/celebrity-news/news/taylor-swift-grants-terminally-ill-4-year-olds-final-wish——watch-201543. Accessed February 18, 2016.

Waddell, Ray. "A Born Headliner." *Billboard* 123 (December 10, 2011), 34. A report on Swift's appeal as a concert attraction. Her promoter, Louis Messina, is quoted as saying that even at the start of her career, she had an "aura" that made her headliner material.

Werde, Bill. "The *Billboard* Q&A: Taylor Swift." *Billboard* 121 (December 19, 2009), 14. Swift discusses hosting *Saturday Night Live*, how her songs represent diary entries, and the awards that she has won.

"What's Driving Acoustic Guitar Sales?" *Music Trades* 162 (October 2014), 54–58. Swift is mentioned as one of the artists associated with the acoustic guitar that seems to be helping to generate an uptick in sales of the instrument.

White, Daniel. "Taylor Swift Partners with Kim Kardashian's Game Designer for New Mobile App." *Time.com* (February 3, 2016), time.com/4207117/taylor-swift-kim-kardashians-mobile-app/?iid=sr-link1. Accessed June 2, 2016. A report that Swift is working with Glu Mobile on a video game for mobile devices.

White, Emily. "Swift, Harris Team for Social Gain." *Billboard* 128 (April 2, 2016), 71. An article about the fact that Swift and boyfriend Calvin Harris experienced gains in social media because they posted photographs of their vacation on Instagram.

Whitten, Sarah. "Taylor Swift Mobile Game to Launch in Late 2016." *CNBC.com* (February 3, 2016), www.cnbc.com/2016/02/03/taylor-swift-mobile-game -to-launch-in-late-2016.html. Accessed February 3, 2016. A report on Glu Mobile's plan to introduce a mobile device game that revolves around Swift.

Widdicombe, Lizzie. "You Belong with Me." *New Yorker* 87 (October 10, 2011), 104–115. An essential feature-length article on Swift, her work, and its effect on Swift's fans.

Willman, Chris. "American Girl." *Entertainment Weekly* 977 (February 8, 2008), 40–43. A feature article on Swift, her use of social media, and the inspirations for her songs.

Willman, Chris. "Big Machine: The First 10 Years." *Billboard* 127 (October 31, 2015), 55–60. A feature article on Big Machine Records and its founder, Scott Borchetta.

Willman, Chris. "Princess Crossover." *New York* 43 (October 18, 2010), 99–101. The author reports on Swift's popularity, the difficulty that past artists had encountered in crossing between the country and pop genres, and the contrast between Swift's material and the repertoire of her elders at a Los Angeles benefit concert for the Country Music Hall of Fame.

Willman, Chris. "Taylor Swift." *Entertainment Weekly* 945 (July 27, 2007), 26. A brief profile of Swift in the wake of her initial success with "Tim McGraw" and her debut album.

Zorian, Lora. Letter to the Editor. *Bitch Magazine: Feminist Response to Popular Culture* 51 (Summer 2011), 4. A response to Rachel McCarthy James's article about Swift. Zorian points to Swift's videos as evidence of the characteristics of strength and female empowerment that her work exhibits.

Index

About the Author

JAMES E. PERONE, PhD, is associate dean of the faculty and the Margaret Morgan Ramsey professor in music at the University of Mount Union, Alliance, Ohio. He holds a master of fine arts in clarinet performance, a master of arts in music theory, and a doctorate in music theory from the State University of New York at Buffalo. He also earned a bachelor of music in music education from Capital University. His published works include the ABC-CLIO titles *Mods, Rockers, and the Music of the British Invasion*; *Music of the Counterculture Era*; *The Words and Music of Elvis Costello*; *Smash Hits: The 100 Songs That Defined America*; and *The Words and Music of Melissa Etheridge*, among others. Perone is also editor of ABC-CLIO's *The Album: A Guide to Pop Music's Most Provocative, Influential, and Important Creations* and series editor of The Praeger Singer-Songwriter Collection.

Printed in the USA
CPSIA information can be obtained
at www.ICGtesting.com
LVHW051611021224
798131LV00003B/37